Overcoming the World: Glory and Shame in [...] sweep of what lies behind John's gospel, i[...] of Israel that speak to the book's theme a[...] world, with fascinating examples of how t[...] by perspective, and perspective is shaped by identity.

One of Yevgeny Ustinovich's strengths is drawing insights from familiar episodes that reframe them in light of the dynamics at play. What the author discovers, from John's perspective, is that humiliation does not necessarily mean dishonour or victimization but can be recast to God's glory – a shift of perspective from man's glory (or his shame) to God's glory.

The apostle John does not simply write of humiliation *followed by* glorification, as true as that is, but suffering itself is transformed. "Jesus was glorified as he goes to the cross. Crucifixion *is* the glorification of the Son of God" (p. 55). Yevgeny Ustinovich helps us to see that if we take John's gospel seriously, we will reconsider the meaning and opportunity of suffering. There is a lot to think about. This book is worth reading and re-reading.

Georges Carillet, DMin
President,
Teaching Ministries International, Florida, USA

Overcoming the World brings gospel hope and comfort to all who are living through challenges of life and relational pains – that is, to so many of us. Yevgeny Ustinovich places John's gospel firmly in the context of rejection and persecution of the early Christians by their own people. His pastoral reading drives home in vivid examples what John's gospel is all about: victory through defeat, conquest through martyrdom, renewal through destruction. The book is structured thematically, and breathes scholarship and authenticity. Troublesome and difficult gospel passages are explained carefully and skillfully by placing them in their historical and literary context. As the Gospel itself, this study aims at a change of perspective for those who are suffering, teaching that the identity of persecuted disciples is in God's glory abiding with them and in them. The ones that were thrown out therefore become the ones that have been sent out into the world that rejected them – commissioned to bring God's message of reconciliation and hope in ever new ways.

Jelle Creemers, PhD
Director, Institute for the Study of Freedom of Religion or Belief,
Evangelische Theologische Faculteit, Leuven, Belgium

Overcoming the World

Langham
GLOBAL LIBRARY

Overcoming the World

Glory and Shame in the Gospel of John

Yevgeny Ustinovich

Langham
GLOBAL LIBRARY

© 2024 Yevgeny Ustinovich

Published 2024 by Langham Global Library
An imprint of Langham Publishing
www.langhampublishing.org

Langham Publishing and its imprints are a ministry of Langham Partnership

Langham Partnership
PO Box 296, Carlisle, Cumbria, CA3 9WZ, UK
www.langham.org

ISBNs:
978-1-83973-927-9 Print
978-1-83973-992-7 ePub
978-1-83973-993-4 PDF

Yevgeny Ustinovich has asserted his right under the Copyright, Designs and Patents Act, 1988 to be identified as the Author of this work.

All rights reserved. No part of this publication may be reproduced, stored in a retrieval system or transmitted, in any form or by any means, electronic, mechanical, photocopying, recording or otherwise, without the prior written permission of the publisher or the Copyright Licensing Agency.

Requests to reuse content from Langham Publishing are processed through PLSclear. Please visit www.plsclear.com to complete your request.

Unless otherwise stated, Scripture quotations are from The Holy Bible, English Standard Version® (ESV®), copyright © 2001 by Crossway, a publishing ministry of Good News Publishers. Used by permission. All rights reserved.

Scripture quotations marked (NIV) are taken from the Holy Bible, New International Version®, NIV®. Copyright © 1973, 1978, 1984, 2011 by Biblica, Inc.™ Used by permission of Zondervan.

British Library Cataloguing-in-Publication Data
A catalogue record for this book is available from the British Library

ISBN: 978-1-83973-927-9

Cover & Book Design: projectluz.com

Langham Partnership actively supports theological dialogue and an author's right to publish but does not necessarily endorse the views and opinions set forth here or in works referenced within this publication, nor can we guarantee technical and grammatical correctness. Langham Partnership does not accept any responsibility or liability to persons or property as a consequence of the reading, use or interpretation of its published content.

Contents

Introduction 1

Part I: "Not of the World"

1 Tribulation in the World 7
2 Where Are We From? 25
3 Where Are We Going? 45
4 The Eyes That See God's Glory 61

Part II: "In the World"

5 Two Kinds of Glory 83
6 The Disciples' Path 105
   Conclusion 121
   Selected Bibliography 125

Introduction

Christianity is by far the most persecuted religion in the world. Every year, thousands of Christians die for their faith, while millions live in places where expressions of this faith are severely limited. For many believers, some of the worst threats of physical and psychological violence come from their own relatives and fellow citizens.

This situation often creates identity problems for the persecuted: "Who am I? Who are we?" These questions may sound hopelessly theoretical – something for the academics who have a lot of time on their hands – but the answers have far-reaching practical consequences. "Who are we if the people closest to us reject us?" In this book, I will try to show how the Gospel of John may become a source of encouragement for Christians who struggle with their identity in cultures where Christianity is less than welcome.

John's gospel can be read on two levels. It is a story of Jesus who was rejected by his own people (John 18:35) because he always sought God's glory (John 8:50). But the text also seems to reflect a story of a persecuted community that survived a painful break with mainstream Judaism. Despite being hurt by the hostile world, this community was sent back into the world to continue Jesus's mission (John 20:21). Disciples of Jesus would accomplish this task in the same way that he did – through the faithful service and patient suffering that lead to God's glory.

Being persecuted is always a traumatic experience. Being persecuted by one's kin may generate a tremendous amount of shame,[1] which makes the situation even worse. How did Jesus solve this problem for his followers? According to Hebrews 12:2, he "endured the cross, despising the shame," but how exactly does it apply to the situations in which his followers – both in the first and twenty-first centuries – often find themselves?

---

1. The words "guilt" and "shame" are often used interchangeably, but it is better to separate them. "Guilt" is usually generated by the awareness of bad things we have said or done, whereas "shame" comes from the things said or done to us. The psychological pain, anxiety, and internal conflict that may result from being labelled as "apostate," "traitor," or "heretic" would belong to this generalized category of "shame." An example illustrating the difference between guilt and shame is considered in chapter 1 (see section titled "The Old Testament: A Torn Prophet for the Torn Nation"): the prophet Isaiah is burdened by guilt because of his own sins and by shame because of the sins of other Israelites.

In part I of this book, I will try to show how John helps his readers to stay rooted in their God-given identity in spite of all the pressure from the hostile world. The reality of their new birth in the Spirit separates them from the mainstream culture in some crucial ways. Believers become free from the expectations of "the world"[2] as they are no longer "of the world" (John 17:16). Through new birth in the Spirit, they have God as their Father (while their persecutors do not), a new destination, a new way of seeing reality, a new place of worship, a new understanding of glory and shame, and a new interpretation of Scripture. The list could go on. The separation is deep; and so great is their freedom that Christians can truly consider themselves dead to the world (Col 3:3).

Yet, this separation is not physical. Jesus prayed, "I do not ask that you take them out of the world, but that you keep them from the evil one" (John 17:15). He sent his disciples back to the world that had rejected him (15:18–20). The physical proximity to scoffers and persecutors gives the church opportunities to witness to the truth the way Jesus did (18:37). In part II, we will look at some ways in which John expected his readers to preach the gospel message to non-believers, particularly those first-century Jews who did not accept Jesus as their Messiah. Being "in the world" means that some events occurring in that world affect both the messengers and their audience.

One of such ground-shattering events was the destruction of Jerusalem in AD 70. All the Jews who lived in the Roman Empire at that time, including followers of Jesus, were shocked by this tragedy. But this situation also presented new possibilities for witnessing to non-messianic Jews. After AD 70, without the temple, Judaism was reinventing itself, and many survivors of the catastrophe were discussing the questions to which John seems to offer his answers: *How does one celebrate Passover and other temple-based holidays? What is to be done about the sacrifices prescribed in the law? And what is the meaning of the Old Testament prophecies that were thought to be related to the Second Temple?* Some of John's answers to these questions will be considered in part II of this book.

Many scholars believe that the Gospel of John was originally written for a group of Jewish believers in Jesus who had been expelled from the synagogue and lost many benefits associated with their status as Jews with synagogue membership.[3] This expulsion and other forms of persecution made them

---

2. The meaning of this term in the Gospel of John is explained in chapter 1 (see section titled "'The World' in the Gospel of John").

3. This is the view held by the majority of Johannine scholars today.

reconsider their identity. Redrawing boundaries is often a painful process, and so there is a lot of anger described in the Fourth Gospel. The vitriolic language used in texts such as John 8:44 have puzzled many commentators. If John sought to convert "the Jews," why did he insult them? In order to solve this riddle, we may have to turn to the OT prophetic tradition. An OT prophet could vilify his audience and threaten them with severe judgement. But when that well-deserved judgement came and everything was destroyed, the prophet would sit among the ruins, mourning with those who mourned, and speak a message of hope. This is what John seems to teach his readers.

The world hates the followers of Jesus. But the world itself is broken, and Jesus's followers are the only ones who have the message of salvation for the world. Jesus overcame the world by suffering what seemed to be the ultimate defeat. He was glorified when he accepted the cross – the most extreme form of rejection and shame. Jesus bids his disciples to follow his path – and the same paradox will be true in their lives as well.

Some of the material in this book is based on the PhD dissertation that I defended in 2019 in the Belgian city of Leuven. Three years later, I left my home country (Ukraine) and came to Belgium again – this time as a refugee. As I was struggling to make sense of my new life here, John's paradoxical teaching on God's glory and the disciples' identity turned out to be one of the best tools that helped me to find direction and hope.

Russia's military and cultural aggression against Ukraine caused, among other things, a deep division in the Russian-speaking evangelical community. It was sad to see some of my colleagues support the aggressor and try to justify the violence against Ukrainians, many of whom are Christians. For Russian-speaking Ukrainians, the conflict cuts very deep. Because of our common language, we used to identify with Russia to some extent, but now that our cultural ties with Russia have been severed, we find ourselves in an unusual and complicated situation. Our experience is not unlike that of the first-century Jewish believers who were excluded from the synagogue.

I do not consider myself persecuted because of my faith. Rather, I went into exile because of my political preferences – identifying with a nation that chose freedom and not with invaders who bring totalitarian rule. But my Christian faith was a major factor in my choosing to identify in this manner. Moreover, some of the reasons Ukraine as a nation learned to cherish freedom had to do with the influence of thousands of Christians who lived, witnessed, and – in times of persecution – suffered for God's glory in that torn country.

As a Bible scholar, I wish I did not have to bring my own traumatic experience into the research; I would very much prefer to focus just on the trials and victories of first-century disciples in the Gospel of John. But when one's life falls apart in such circumstances, it is impossible to prevent these circumstances from influencing the way we read the Scriptures. This experience of a torn life cannot be simply ignored, and the responsible way to deal with it is to be aware that it influences our interpretation of Scripture and then carry on. Jesus's promise of freedom for those who abide in his word (John 8:31–32) extends to refugees too.

It is my hope and prayer that this book will help readers reflect on this liberating truth and, through studying the Gospel of John, strengthen suffering Christians on their way to the fullness of joy.

Part I

"Not of the World"

1

Tribulation in the World

"In the world you will have tribulation. But take heart; I have overcome the world" (John 16:33). Jesus spoke these words the night before his cruel death. Their meaning is not obvious. What kind of victory did Jesus have in mind? Why did he speak about this victory as something already accomplished?

"The World" in the Gospel of John

Before attempting to answer these questions, it would be helpful to clarify what the term "the world" (ὁ κόσμος, *ho kosmos*) meant for John. This word is used seventy-eight times throughout his gospel. It is found at the beginning of the book (1:9–10), in its last verse (21:25), and in many passages in between. Clearly, this word was important for John; and while it has a broad range of possible meanings, some of those meanings shape a characteristically Johannine "accent."

The World Is Made by God

The first thing a reader needs to know about the world is that it is God's creation. This truth may seem so obvious to some commentators that they take it for granted and hurry on to describe other specifically Johannine features of "the world." Yet, failure to remember the simple truth that the world is God's creation may lead to huge misunderstandings.

Because the world was created by the good God, it was good, even "very good" (Gen 1:31) – at least in the beginning. As a result of the fall, evil entered the world, and the evil one has power over the world (1 John 5:19). Yet, the world is not beyond the hope of redemption. The last book of the Bible promises that God will make all things new and introduces the reader to a perfect world, where there is no sin, no curse, no death, and no suffering (Rev 21:4–5). That world is going to be very different from the one we live in – to put it in theological language, there will be much discontinuity. Yet, it will not be a completely different world, inhabited by creatures that have nothing to do with our world; rather, it will be the present world redeemed.

When God makes the new heaven and the new earth, this will not just be an act of God the Creator but also the final glorious act of God the Redeemer. If God simply damned the old world, destroyed it, and created a new one, there would be no redemption to speak about. Yet, there is some continuity between the present dark world and the glorious world to come. The Lamb of God overcame the world by taking away the sin of the world (John 1:29).

In John's understanding of the world, there is both continuity and discontinuity, which makes interpreting the Fourth Gospel a difficult but fascinating task. The world is torn between its present misery and its future glory.

The World Depends on God

According to John, the world in its present state is alienated from God and in active rebellion against God. The world "hates" those who are sent into the world from God (John 15:18–19). Yet, God did not give up on the world (3:16). He has a solution for the sin of the world (1:29), although this solution will be beyond anyone's expectations. To help his readers understand the paradoxical relationship between God and the world, John often uses irony.[1] "And this is the judgement: the light has come into the world, and people loved the darkness rather than the light because their works were evil. For everyone who does wicked things hates the light and does not come to the light, lest his works should be exposed" (3:19–20). People are afraid of light because it brings exposure and shame. So, they try to hide in the darkness and, by so doing, bring judgement on themselves. This sad irony results from the world's ontological dependence on God. The world needs God but does not want him, and the world wants something that it does not need. According to Koester,

> John's Gospel recognizes that human beings are complex and subject to conflicting impulses. Some passages describe thirsty people, who have a need for the life that comes from God and

---

1. The word "irony" is used here in a broad sense – as contrasting reality and expectations.

who search for something to meet this need. Hunger reflects a similar idea, and the Gospel shows how the hunger to overcome one's separation from the source of life can produce a misguided impulse to fix attention on material gifts rather than on the divine giver. Darkness depicts people embracing what alienates them from God, turning the lack of knowledge into a new certainty and unbelief into a new faith. People are both estranged from and attracted to God. They need what they reject, yet have a propensity to reject what they need.[2]

When readers meet various characters in the Fourth Gospel – and in their own lives – it is helpful to keep in mind that many of them experience this tension of wanting something that they do not really need. Jesus was aware of people's true needs since he knew even the deepest thoughts of their hearts (2:25; 6:15), and he understood their true condition. When he said, for example, "I am the bread of life" (6:35), this implies that the world by itself cannot preserve its own life. As much as the world hates the source of its own existence, it is still dependent on this source. So how can someone who is "of the world" receive life if they do not *want* it (see, for example, 5:40)? This is a cruel dilemma for a human being, but it is also a dilemma for God because he seeks to save the world. God's solution to this dilemma is "ironic," as we will see in the following chapters.

The World Includes Both the Jews and the Gentiles

John's treatment of the world's condition defies simplistic, black-and-white descriptions. In some passages, however, his language seems to almost invite such an approach. John does rely heavily on contrast: light and darkness, love and hate, life and death. He shows no scruples when it comes to boundaries – the community of God's children (1:12–13) is very different from the crowd whose father is the devil (8:44). Many of John's contemporaries would have approved of such a distinction. What they would not have anticipated is the way the lines are sometimes drawn – that is, the criteria by which some people are "in" and some are "out."

Most Jews in John's day seemed to have been aware of the tension between Israel and the hostile gentile world. The former were often pictured as dry land and the latter as the roaring sea that threatened to overwhelm God's people.

---

2. Koester, *Word of Life*, 65.

It is from the sea that the monsters emerge in both Daniel's and John's visions (Dan 7:3; Rev 13:1).[3]

One of the surprising features of John's gospel is that the boundaries between "the Jews" and "the world" seem to fade away. The Son of God was rejected by "the world" represented by "the Jews": "He was in the world, and the world was made through him, yet the world did not know him. He came to his own, and his own people did not receive him" (1:10–11).

When Jesus told the disciples that the world hated both him and them, this may seem like an exaggeration to modern readers. After all, most people in the world have nothing to do with persecuting Christians. Those religious fanatics who kill followers of Jesus do not represent the whole world, do they? After all, there was more to the (ancient) world than the Pharisees and Sadducees.

While John was perfectly aware of this complex dynamic, he notes that Christ's message causes division among the people (7:43). He does not paint with a broad brush, but nor does he allow Jesus's persecutors to be represented as just a marginal group. For example, in his description of the dealings between "the Jews"[4] and Pilate, he shows how religious fanatics were able to manipulate even the Roman governor, a man who commanded legions. It does sound extraordinary, but it is true – the mightiest man in the province ended up trying to please Jesus's persecutors. While many non-Christians in our world do not feel hatred but, rather, sympathy towards Jesus, John's theology of persecution is not based on their feelings. John shows that persecution comes from the very essence of the world. Pilate did not have anything against Jesus personally – until he found himself under pressure. The world knows how to use coercion and manipulation when it comes to persecuting Christ and Christians. When Jesus said, "I am the light of the world" (8:12), one can infer from this statement that the world by itself, without Jesus, is a very dark place.

Jesus came to "his own" – to Israel – and "his own" rejected him (1:11). This does not, however, signal defeat for Jesus, who, in the course of his ministry, changed and reconfigured the group called "his own." When he was about to leave the world, it is the disciples who are called "his own" (13:1). This

---

3. When it comes to the authorship of John and Revelation, I hold what used to be a majority view in the history of the church but is a minority view now: both the Fourth Gospel and the book of Revelation were written by the apostle John. This will probably not be a great hurdle for those readers who do not accept this position since even the most sceptical commentators usually admit that there is a remarkable unity of thought between John and Revelation and so both books, whoever the authors were, must have come from the same circle.

4. Quotation marks here help emphasize that we are dealing with specific individuals who lived in the first century and persecuted Christians. John's vitriolic comments about "the Jews" cannot (and must not) be irresponsibly projected to Jews outside of that first-century context.

distinction between insiders and outsiders remains, but while that distinction is very sharp,[5] it does not correspond any longer to the distinction between Israel and Gentiles. Some of "the Jews," in spite of belonging to the chosen people, ended up walking away into the darkness;[6] and some "Greeks," even though coming from a pagan culture, were drawn to Jesus. Following Jesus – both in the first century and the twenty-first century – means that the boundaries of the "in" group to which followers belong will be changed, often in unexpected ways.

The World Hates Christ and His Disciples

"God loves you and offers a wonderful plan for your life."[7] These are the opening words of a well-known outline to present the gospel in the modern world. These words summarize much of the gospel message and emphasize the need for a personal response to the message. In some cases, however, this summary needs to be elaborated on because it can be – and sometimes has been – misunderstood in some contexts. To decrease the risk of such misunderstanding, I would suggest a short addition to this summary – something like this: "God loves you and has a wonderful plan for your life. But this plan includes suffering – suffering that leads to God's glory. Because of that suffering, many people reject God's plan and substitute it with their own plans, and this may lead to an even worse kind of suffering."

The good news preached to the hostile world comes at the cost of much suffering – both for Christ himself and for the church that proclaims the good news. The theme of psychological and physical violence is developed throughout the Fourth Gospel. Jesus was insulted, slandered, threatened, mocked, flogged, and crucified. He also warned his disciples that "the world" would treat them in much the same way. They would be hated, persecuted, and, eventually, murdered (15:18–20; 16:2). In the prologue to his gospel, John describes how the world rejected the Son of God (1:11); in the epilogue, he records the prediction of martyrdom for one of Jesus's followers (21:19). The way to God's glory is through suffering – for both Jesus and his disciples.

One of the ways the disciples would be persecuted was by expulsion from the synagogue. Compared to intense forms of physical violence such as

---

5. Although it is not absolute, the image of "the door of the sheep" (John 10:7) means that outsiders still have an opportunity to come in and join the flock.

6. See John 13:30.

7. See for example: https://www.cru.org/us/en/how-to-know-god/would-you-like-to-know-god-personally.html.

crucifixion, this type of trial may often be overlooked or underestimated. But acknowledging this kind of persecution was very important for John, and it may also be important for some modern readers. The word translated literally "put out of the synagogue" (ἀποσυνάγωγος, *aposynagogos*), is used only three times in the entire body of ancient Greek literature available to scholars. All three uses of this self-explanatory term occur in the Gospel of John (9:22; 12:42; 16:2). There are also instances where exclusion from the synagogue is implied, even though the term itself is not used (see 9:34).

A reader from an individualistic and secularized culture – as in the West today – may fail to fully grasp the painful aspects of this social reality. Christians in the Majority World, on the other hand, know quite well that exclusion from corporate worship in a collectivistic, deeply religious society brings social and economic hardship. The outcasts – those who do not fit in with an established religion – are often refused employment, business opportunities,[8] medical care, and may even be denied protection from mob violence and other forms of injustice.

At the end of the first century AD, one of the hardest trials the church faced came as a result of the requirement for emperor worship. Christians who refused to participate in that idolatrous rite were viewed as traitors and executed. Although the Jews were exempt from sacrificing to the emperor because their religion was officially recognized, this exemption did not seem to apply to those Jews who had been denied membership in the synagogue. So, the excommunicated often faced a dilemma: sacrifice to Caesar or be martyred. No wonder John refers to some Jewish communities in Asia Minor as "synagogue[s] of Satan" (Rev 2:9; 3:9).

Even in those cases where excommunication did not necessarily involve physical violence, the consequences of this "social death" were still painful. In this book, I focus mainly on the psychological suffering caused by the problem of torn identity. John's original audience probably struggled with these questions: *If we are excommunicated from the mainstream Jewish religion, can we still consider ourselves Jews? And if we can, is our Jewishness something to be proud of or ashamed of? After all, most of the Jews in the first century rejected Jesus. What does this say about Israel as a whole?*

This approach of focusing on the psychological suffering of those who experience physical violence and deprivation may seem artificial, therapeutic, and very Western. But it is not. In the chapters that follow, I will try to show that the issue of identity is extremely important for John. When the question

---

8. See Revelation 13:17.

"Who are we?" is given a scriptural answer, it relieves us from a heavy burden. When Christians are able to resolve the internal conflict caused by belonging to a culture where the gospel is not always welcomed, they are free to follow Christ in a much more confident and joyful way.

In the next section, I will show how this internal conflict – belonging to a nation going through a time of apostasy – was resolved in the life of the biblical prophet Isaiah and why Isaiah's message was so relevant for John.

The Old Testament: A Torn Prophet for the Torn Nation

In the last several decades, much has been said about John's alleged "anti-Semitism." Although this is a strange charge to bring against someone who was himself a Jew, in the post-Holocaust world, one cannot simply ignore, for example, Jesus's words, "You are of your father the devil" (John 8:44). This and other passages in the Gospel of John have sometimes been abused by wicked people. But the gospels themselves present no justification for any form of racial hatred unless one makes three exegetical mistakes: (1) ignoring the original context of the gospel as a whole; 2) ignoring the historical and social milieu in which the gospels were written; or 3) ignoring the literal context of the gospels – especially the continuity between the prophetic texts of the Old Testament and the gospels in the New Testament. Here, I will briefly explain how the first two mistakes can be avoided; then I will deal, in more detail, with the third factor.

Modern readers may cringe as they come across those passages in the Fourth Gospel where "the Jews" are portrayed in a rather negative light – as stubborn, ignorant, and aggressive. However, a closer look at this gospel reveals that such an impression is seriously flawed. John mentions that there is division among the people – some are willing to listen to Christ, while others keep rejecting him (10:19–21). Jesus himself identifies rather strongly with "the Jews" and teaches about their unique role in the history of salvation (4:22). A comprehensive study of John's use of the term "the Jews" reveals many positive connotations – "the Jews" have a rich spiritual heritage. The good news is that they can lay claim to this heritage even after the destruction of the temple. In Jesus, benefits promised in the OT become available to those who believe.

In the Gospel of John, coming to faith is often shown as a crisis through which the believer's life undergoes a radical change. To appreciate the nature of this crisis, one has to keep in mind not only the insults against "the Jews" but also the praise associated with them.[9] The chosen people had always lived in a state of tension between the blessings and the curses promised in the law (Deuteronomy 28), and this tension creates much of the identity conflict seen in the Fourth Gospel.

The second factor that needs to be considered is the historical and social context. After the destruction of the temple, the question "Whose fault is it?" was hotly debated in the diaspora communities. Josephus[10] blamed the Zealots, using such abusive language that John's insults directed against "the Jews" seem mild in comparison.[11] Some rabbis blamed the *am-haaretz* (the people) – that is, the uneducated masses who did not have adequate knowledge of the law. Others pointed fingers at the elites, including the high-priestly clans who cooperated with the Romans and failed to prevent the catastrophe. These are all instances of Jews vilifying other Jews for the perceived failure to live according to the true calling and identity of the Jewish people.

When John, being a Jew himself, criticized "the Jews" for not being faithful to their own law, he was only doing what many of his contemporaries did after AD 70. But he also followed the OT prophets who castigated their own nation in ways that may shock modern sensibilities.

John's use of the OT prophets is a theme that has been studied a lot lately. Here, I highlight his literary relationship with only one such prophet – Isaiah. In chapter 12, when John gives a summary of Jesus's entire earthly ministry, he quotes Isaiah twice and adds his own commentary on the second quotation:

> Therefore they could not believe. For again Isaiah said,
>
> "He has blinded their eyes
>   and hardened their heart,

---

9. The very first mention of a person's ethnic identity in the Gospel of John is connected with praise. Jesus spoke highly of Nathanael's openness and honesty – qualities of a true Israelite (1:47). Some readers may be quite surprised by the fact that the Son of God praised a fallen human being who did not even have (as yet) a saving faith. Being an Israelite is seen as a good thing; those "Jews" who were called children of the devil (8:44) and insulted in other ways simply did not live according to their Jewish identity.

10. Flavius Josephus was a first-century Jewish historian and an eyewitness of the war against Rome. He was even one of the leaders of the rebellion but later defected to Rome and became a slave of the Roman commander Vespasian.

11. "[T]hey were the slaves, the scum, and the spurious and abortive offspring of our nation, while they overthrew the city themselves, and forced the Romans, whether they would or no, to gain a melancholy reputation, by acting gloriously against them, and did almost draw that fire upon the temple" (Josephus, *J.W.* 5.10.5).

lest they see with their eyes,
       and understand with their heart,
and turn, and I would heal them."

Isaiah said these things because he saw his [Jesus's] glory and spoke of him. (John 12:39–41)

John was referring to a well-known passage about Isaiah's vision and calling (Isaiah 6). In that encounter, the prophet was both separated (set aside) from his fellow Israelites – what John might call "the world" – and sent back to them. God's twofold action – separation and sending – is both efficient and painful.

In the year of King Uzziah's death, Isaiah saw the Lord enthroned above[12] the temple.[13] He also saw the seraphim who praise this holy God, but he could not join them in their worship. Failure to praise the Lord in his presence would have been seen as an insult, but if Isaiah had tried to praise him, it would have been much worse. His attempts to glorify God would only have defiled the temple: "And I said: 'Woe is me! For I am lost; for I am a man of unclean lips, and I dwell in the midst of a people of unclean lips; for my eyes have seen the King, the LORD of hosts!'" (Isa 6:5).

Confronted with God's holiness, Isaiah recognized his own sinfulness. He could only agree that a death sentence for him would be just. The uncleanness Isaiah refers to resulted from his sin. This is similar to the ritual uncleanness described in the law of Moses: an Israelite who defiled himself would not be allowed to worship in the temple (Lev 11:24–28). Presuming to do so was an offence against God's holiness (Lev 7:20).

Isaiah realized that sin can defile people in an even worse way. But why was his attention concentrated on "lips"? It is not that Isaiah was focusing on some specific sin or some specific area of sin in his life. Rather, he was aware of the "liturgical" dimension of sin. "If one turns away his ear from hearing the law, even his prayer is an abomination" (Prov 28:9).

The prophet acknowledges the crushing burden of guilt, but there is also something else. He was also overcome by shame – shame for his own nation: "and I dwell in the midst of a people of unclean lips" (Isa 6:5). He knew that Israel had not lived up to its glorious calling, but he did not separate himself from his fellow citizens. We can all feel guilt for the things we have said and done, but we can also feel shame for the things said and done to us.

---

12. An important detail for this prophet was the fact that God is too big to reside inside a structure made by human beings (Isa 66:1).

13. Acts 22:17.

Confession of sin leads to forgiveness and cleansing: "Then one of the seraphim flew to me, having in his hand a burning coal that he had taken with tongs from the altar. And he touched my mouth and said: 'Behold, this has touched your lips; your guilt is taken away, and your sin atoned for'" (Isa 6:6–7). After that, Isaiah was sent to Israel. The nation would be cleansed in much the same way the prophet was – through fire and burning coals. This would be an extremely painful process for, in order to be renewed and purified, Jerusalem had to be burned and led into captivity (6:11–13).

Having been forgiven and set free from guilt through the sacrifice – the burning coal that was taken from the altar – Isaiah could stand without shame before God. But shame did not disappear from his life altogether. As the prophet preached to the people whose hearts were hardened, he would often do things normally considered shameful (see Isa 20:2–4). What has changed here is the set of criteria by which what is shameful is distinguished from what is glorious.

Soon after this vision the temple was probably once again filled with "people of unclean lips" – visitors who thought they were praising God. Isaiah shames them for that and for many other sinful practices (1:12–17). He does it a lot. He still identifies with Israel but now he identifies with it as with a mission field or, to use his own metaphor, a "vineyard" (5:1).

Although preachers often encourage their audiences to "love the sinner, hate the sin," sometimes it is quite difficult to discern the fine line separating the sinner's "self" from their sin. One reason for this difficulty is that sin has to do with one's identity – it involves promoting a false "self" and being (or trying to be) someone other than who God designed you to be. When speaking to Israelites who had failed to live according to Yahweh's ways, Isaiah sometimes mockingly refuses to acknowledge them as Israelites: "Hear the word of the LORD, you rulers of Sodom! Give ear to the teaching of our God, you people of Gomorrah!" (1:10). In the prophet's cultural context, it would have been hard to come up with a worse insult. Yet, such insults do not indicate the end of a conversation. In fact, they are used as an invitation to a very difficult dialogue.

In another passage, using phrases that may seem like conversation killers to a modern reader but are, in fact, conversation openers, Isaiah questions (metaphorically) the origin of his antagonists: "But you, draw near, sons of the sorceress, offspring of the adulterer and the loose woman. Whom are you mocking? Against whom do you open your mouth wide and stick out your tongue? Are you not children of transgression, the offspring of deceit [?]" (Isa 57:3–4). The prophet calls his opponents illegitimate children, thus denying them any rights to Israel's heritage (Deut 23:2) and any privileges of the covenant. In the Gospel of John Jesus will use much the same language with a similar purpose (John 8:44). It sounds cruel, and it is meant to. The spiritual state of Isaiah's contemporaries was so woeful that only "shock therapy" could heal them.

Perhaps a modern concept may help us understand Israel's and Isaiah's dilemma a bit better. At the end of the twentieth century, political scientists began to use the term "torn country." This expression, coined by Samuel Huntington, was used to describe societies that were caught between their pro-Western aspirations and their non-Western values and lifestyles.[14] If this concept can also be applied to studying ancient societies, Israel in the time of Isaiah can certainly be described as a torn nation – torn between its unique calling (Exod 19:5–6) and its apostasy. Isaiah does not describe this conflict as a detached observer but as someone who was personally involved in the situation. He was a torn man because he belonged to a nation that had rejected his message. Thus, there is much anger and sarcasm in his offensive language. He preached to a people who did not want what they needed, people who loved what ought to be hated and hated what is worthy of love.

Isaiah's prophecies also contain a message of hope. A wonderful child, who would bring peace, would be born (Isa 9:6–7). A suffering servant of Yahweh, who would restore Israel's relationship with God, would come (52:13–53:12). Many of Isaiah's prophecies have been fulfilled in Jesus's life and death, and there are many parallels between Jesus's ministry and Isaiah's experience. By placing the quote from Isaiah 6 in the crucial transitional passage – at the end of the first half of his gospel – John seems to address the situation of his original audience as well. In fact, Jesus's whole mission builds on Isaiah's prophecies and expands their scope. The same dynamic – torn messenger for a torn people – was present both in his life and in the lives of his disciples.

The New Testament: A Torn Saviour for the Torn World

The Fourth Gospel often depicts Jesus as being present at the centre of violent conflicts. He was frequently in situations where the expression "torn individual" would seem an applicable description. His own brothers did not believe in him (7:5); his disciples often misunderstood him (14:8); his fellow Jews opposed him; the rulers snubbed him and challenged his authority; his trusted disciple denied him (18:15–18; 25–27) and even a person he healed turned out to be totally ungrateful (5:15). At the end of his earthly life, Jesus was betrayed by

---

14. Huntington, *Clash of Civilizations*, 138.

one of his own disciples (13:18), abandoned by his friends, and disowned by "[his] own nation" (18:35).

In some passages in the Synoptic Gospels, Jesus is shown as experiencing an inner conflict. For example, he predicted the destruction of Jerusalem – an event that took place in AD 70 – and stated, in no ambiguous terms, that this would be God's judgement on the unfaithful city (Luke 21:20–22). There is nothing unjust about God's "vengeance," but such predictions did not fill Jesus with joy; in fact, he wept over the city and the victims who would be trapped inside during the siege (Luke 19:41–44).

One could list many more examples of how Jesus experienced seemingly contradictory emotions because of his complicated relationship with Israel. Along with Isaiah and other OT prophets, Jesus could also be called a "torn person"; yet, on some deeper level, he was not. The inner conflict he may have experienced in living among people who both praised and rejected him did not affect the core of his identity – his understanding of himself as being in perfect union with the Father.

Limitations of space do not allow me to treat this theme in greater detail. I will only address one of the most common objections to the statement made in the previous paragraph. This objection has to do with the cry of dereliction that was heard on the cross: "My God, my God, why have you forsaken me?" (Matt 27:46). Does this not show, the objection runs, that Jesus's perfect union with the Father was broken at some point during the crucifixion? In responding to this objection, I will also try to show how the Gospel of John may help us understand some difficult passages in the Synoptic Gospels.

When we meditate on Jesus's suffering, we are confronted with a deeper mystery, which should make us more aware of our limitations. We must take off our shoes as we tread this holy ground and readily acknowledge that there is much here that we cannot understand. It would be wise to refrain from easy answers. Yet, this does not mean that we cannot be certain about anything at all. There are points on which Scripture is quite clear. One such point is Jesus's own interpretation of the cross. As he said in John 10:17–18: "For this reason the Father loves me, because I lay down my life that I may take it up again. No one takes it from me, but I lay it down of my own accord. I have authority to lay it down, and I have authority to take it up again. This charge I have received from my Father."[15]

---

15. I will return to this text in chapter 3 (see section titled "Jesus's Death: Not a Tragedy") and try to show how these words bring encouragement to persecuted believers.

In the Synoptic Gospels, Jesus also predicted – more than once – his death and resurrection (see Mark 8:31). He is depicted as freely choosing to go to the cross. Moreover, he seems to have had an opportunity to abort the execution and summon the aid of twelve legions of angels (Matt 26:53), but he did not do so – not even when his enemies mockingly suggested that he save himself (Matt 27:42–43). Thus, everything that happened to Jesus on the cross – including the terrible moment when God abandoned him (Matt 27:46) – happened through his own choice. He went through this indescribable horror knowing that God would vindicate him.

On the cross, Jesus's cry of dereliction is a quotation of the opening words of Psalm 22, and these words were misunderstood by those who stood at the cross (Matt 27:47). These soldiers were by no means the only ones who misinterpreted the meaning of Jesus's cry of dereliction. Almost two thousand years later, Albert Schweitzer, for example, thought that these words expressed utter disappointment. According to Schweitzer, Jesus had hoped that God would deliver him but, when that expectation proved false, died as a failed and deeply disillusioned prophet. Unlike the high priests and other spectators at Calvary, Schweitzer did not taunt Jesus; yet, just like them, he viewed the crucifixion as a failure. Many of our contemporaries hold similar views, with the passion of Christ often perceived as some kind of tragedy rather than as victory over the world.[16]

The gospels themselves do not leave much room for such an interpretation of the cross. By citing Psalm 22, Jesus showed that several OT prophecies were being fulfilled. Since it was agonizingly difficult for someone who was being crucified to speak, every phrase Jesus uttered from the cross had to be as short as possible. But the evangelists indicate that Jesus was referring to the whole psalm, not just to its first line. The soldiers divided Jesus's clothes among themselves (John 19:23–24) by casting lots. The spectators taunted him, repeating, almost verbatim, words from this psalm (Ps 22:8; Matt 27:43). The details of the crucifixion correspond in a remarkable way to the metaphorical description given by David.[17]

---

16. Chapter 3 (section titled "Jesus's Death: Not a Tragedy") contains a detailed discussion on how this flawed perception of the cross has resulted in many modern people failing to understand the suffering of the church in the world.

17. David himself, as far as we know, never had his hands and feet literally pierced (Ps 22:16). This metaphor most likely involves poetic exaggeration that helped David to express his feeling of helplessness that resulted from a loss of control. He had lost his status overnight – going from the king's son-in-law to a fugitive who had been robbed of all his possessions. Even his wife had been given to another man (1 Sam 25:44). After that, David endured several other situations involving loss of property and loss of dignity. Yet, in the messianic interpretation

Psalm 22 predicts details such as gambling over the Messiah's[18] garments, mocking him, putting his bones out of joint, his severe thirst, pierced hands and feet. Predictions related to all these details were fulfilled during the crucifixion. But the psalm does not end there. Its second half describes the deliverance that results in blessing on a global, cosmic scale: "All the ends of the earth shall remember and turn to the LORD, and all the families of the nations shall worship before you" (22:27). In these words, we hear an echo of the great promise made to Abraham: "and in you all the families of the earth shall be blessed" (Gen 12:3). This great blessing has to do with the Messiah's suffering and his reign (Ps 22:28).

The Gospel of John has much to say about this relationship between Christ's suffering and glory. John carefully describes prophecies from Psalm 22 that were fulfilled during the crucifixion. But that fulfilment did not end with Jesus's death. The night before his execution, when Jesus washed the disciples' feet, he called them "friends" (John 15:14), which seemed to reveal a new dimension in their relationship. When the risen Christ met Mary Magdalene, he sent her to the disciples, now referred to by Jesus as "my brothers" (20:17). Later on that day, he came to them and stood in their midst – most likely an allusion to Psalm 22:22: "I will tell of your name to my brothers; in the midst of the congregation I will praise you" (see also Heb 2:12).

Like any human being, Jesus experienced sorrow and anguish (John 11:38; 12:27), and the passion narrative shows that he underwent unimaginable suffering. Yet, this suffering did not destroy the core of his identity. He always knew who he was and that his identity was rooted in the love of the Father who had sent him and not in what the world did to him. Being anchored in his God-given identity helped Jesus to endure and overcome an enormous amount of physical pain and psychological suffering, including rejection and shame.

John wanted his Christian readers to be rooted in a similar understanding of who they were – sons and daughters of the Father and disciples who were sent into the hostile world. Understanding our new identity in Christ is not an academic exercise but one of the chief means of encouragement for a

---

provided by the NT authors, these laments are far more than just expressions of feelings – they are prophetic descriptions of future events and, to that extent, they are accurate.

18. In the OT, David is often called God's anointed. "Messiah" is the Hellenized (and later anglicized) form of the Hebrew word meaning "the anointed [one]." While in Christian usage this word is normally reserved for Jesus, there is (technically) nothing wrong in applying it to David and other OT characters – including the patriarchs (Ps 105:15) and even the gentile king Cyrus (Isa 45:1) – who are said to be "anointed" by God. Since there was no difference between Hebrew lower-case and upper-case letters, we could put it this way: the psalms describe the suffering and victory of *a* messiah who is a prototype of *the* Messiah.

community that is suffering because of the world's hatred (15:18–19) and will, most probably, suffer even more. This strong sense of identity will also help contemporary Christians who suffer physical and psychological violence at the hands of their own relatives, compatriots, or (former) coreligionists.

Being rejected by "one's own" – to use John's language – may generate a strong sense of shame. Sooner or later, Jewish believers who had been expelled from a synagogue had to struggle with these questions: "Who are we now after all this has been done to us?" and "Are we still Jewish?" John's answer is based on a paradox: we are still Jewish, while our persecutors have lost the right to call themselves "Jews." While this is most clearly stated in the book of Revelation (2:9; 3:9), this loss of Jewish identity is also implied in the Fourth Gospel – for example, in the passage where "the Jews," represented by the chief priests, declare their loyalty to Caesar (19:15), forming a striking contrast with OT texts that glorify God as king (Ps 10:16) and speak of Israel as his "treasured possession" (Exod 19:5–6).

Seeking to encourage believers who had been excommunicated from the synagogue, John "excommunicates" the synagogue – excludes its leaders and members from the messianic blessings. He can do this because it had been done before by OT prophets. The debate on who is "in" and who is "out" is, in the long run, a debate on the issue of authority – in other words, who can make such decisions? It is here that we see Johannine irony at its best: the risen Christ comes to a group of traumatized and marginalized disciples, who keep their doors locked "for fear of the Jews" (20:19), and gives them this kind of authority, and now that the Holy Spirit acts through these disciples, they can decide who will or will not belong to the community of forgiven sinners (20:23).[19]

In the next chapter, we will look, in more detail, at how John accomplishes this reversal. A person's identity must contain answers to at least three worldview questions: "Who am I?," "Where do I come from?," and "Where am I going?" John's answers, when properly understood, bring great encouragement to a suffering community. According to the Fourth Evangelist, the members of this community are "children of God" (1:12) who have been given eternal life and will witness Christ's glory (17:3, 24). These truths both separate them from the world and prepare them to be sent into the world.

---

19. See chapter 2, page 26 for a fuller exploration of this verse.

Summary

"For God so loved the world . . ." (John 3:16). Since this statement describes some very complicated aspects of reality, it defies simplistic explanations. "The world" in the Gospel of John is a dark place; "the world" rebels against God and hates his messengers – including Jesus and the disciples whom he sent to continue his mission. God's love for "the world" is not sentimental. He will renew "the world," but in a paradoxical kind of way. "The world" cannot be gradually improved by progress; nor can it be reconciled to God without some catastrophic events – and without a sacrifice of cosmic significance.

God's love sent Jesus, and Jesus conquered "the world" (16:33). "The world" was made for God's glory, but it seeks to be independent from God and tries to glorify itself. This is why, in order to be saved, "the world" needs to be conquered by someone who seeks God's glory. That conquest is not what most people might expect. Jesus conquered through martyrdom; he overcame by dying – and being raised from the dead. This pattern – victory through defeat – can be traced throughout the Bible.

"The world" is torn between light and darkness, between its dependence on God and its striving for autonomy. "The world" does not want what it needs – which is to be reconciled with God – and does not need what it wants – to glorify itself. The world is torn between its original glorious purpose and its present miserable state. God's solution for this torn world is ironic in an awesome kind of way. God chose a special nation – Israel – that prepared the world for the conquest by Jesus.

Israel also turned out to be a torn nation, and the conflict between its glorious destiny and its unfaithfulness is present throughout much of the OT. Can God fulfil his plan in spite of Israel's torn state? The answer given by the OT prophets exceeds all expectations: God will fulfil his plan – not so much *in spite of* Israel's torn identity as *through* it. God would renew Israel through defeat and destruction.

To preach this message of paradoxical renewal, God sent prophets who were also torn individuals. These prophets were often treated with contempt because their fellow Israelites failed to understand what true glory is. When the nation spiralled down towards defeat and captivity, righteousness brought shame and wickedness brought approval. Prophets like Isaiah interacted with their contemporaries in a way that included exchanging insults and other expressions of anger or resentment.

In the Gospel of John, this prophetic tradition continues with Jesus, in a situation similar to the one the OT prophets had to deal with before the Babylonian captivity. John's original readers, who lived after the fall of

Jerusalem and the destruction of the Second Temple (AD 70), were not unlike the Israelites who were scattered after the destruction of the First Temple. If the Gospel of John is separated from its historical context – that is, the first-century Roman Empire – and its literal context – that is, its continuity with the OT prophetic texts – interpretative fallacies are practically inevitable, especially when one tries to understand the insults Jesus hurled at his opponents. But when Jesus's words are properly contextualized, they can be interpreted as part of his ministry that brings healing and restoration.

2

Where Are We From?

Jesus separates his faithful followers from the world, yet this separation is spiritual, not physical. He separates them from the world and then sends them back into the world. Although the world will treat them just like it treated him, the world can do nothing about the new identity that Jesus gives his followers. Some of John's first readers had already been rejected by the world. That rejection often took very specific forms and was communicated by their own families and religious leaders. A person who has been physically beaten needs time to recover physically. When someone has been hurt by betrayal or other forms of psychological violence, that trauma also takes time to heal. People whose social status has been greatly diminished because of their faithfulness to God need to have that status restored. This is a genuine need of a person created in the image of God, and the Bible takes that need seriously.[1]

The Gospel of John offers hope to those who have been treated as outcasts. Having drawn the disciples out of the world towards himself, Jesus then sent them back into the world. Yet, that movement "into the world" is also a movement towards Jesus – and I will deal with this paradox in chapter 3 (section titled "Jesus's Death: Not a Tragedy") and chapter 6 (section titled "Sent by the One Sent by the Father"). The disciples grew closer to Jesus when they were cast out of the synagogue – to put this in the context of the modern world, when they were cast out from other social groups that formerly provided protection, nourishment, guidance, and a sense of belonging. The disciples abide in Jesus even as they are sent into the world (John 15:4).

---

1. For example, when Israel's ambassadors were treated shamefully by the Ammonites, David recognized their need for healing and restoration (2 Sam 10:5).

New Birth: The Source of Identity and Conflicts

Before sending the disciples into the world, Jesus dealt with their trauma. In the Gospel of John, he restored them when he appeared to them in person (20:19–23); yet, he also promised that those who believed without seeing him would be blessed (20:29). He gave his disciples the Holy Spirit and empowered them with authority to forgive sins and to refuse forgiveness where there was no repentance (20:22–23).

This verse (20:23) has had a difficult history of interpretation, going back to the time of the Reformation. The Roman Catholic Church insisted that Jesus, in this passage, formally instituted a sacrament of penance so that properly ordained priests – whose authority is said to derive from the apostles – could give absolution on behalf of God. The Protestants had their own counterarguments, which we do not need to discuss here. However, it is important that Reformation-related theological controversies do not keep us from focusing on the original context. The Reformation-era debates around that verse had to do with the church's role in the lives of people who were already Christians but needed help in their struggles with sin. The original context, however, had to do with the church's mission to the world and the great difference between those who follow Christ and those who do not.

Jesus makes his disciples a community of resurrection, a community of the Holy Spirit, and a community of forgiveness. In the original context in which John wrote, forgiveness of sins was a painful and confusing subject for many. The Jerusalem Temple, the only place where it was permissible to make sin offerings, was gone. Of the survivors of the tragedy of AD 70, some groups believed that forgiveness of sins could be obtained through studying the Torah and doing good deeds – which is the most popular opinion in Judaism nowadays. Others hoped to re-establish the temple cult through armed rebellion. And there were also those who sought to develop some new rituals and traditions to replace temple worship. Yet none of these options seemed to have a solid scriptural foundation.

John's solution to the problem of sin is quite different. In the very first chapter of his gospel, he introduces the "Lamb of God" (1:29) – an extremely important concept for those Jews who longed to return to temple worship – and repeatedly stresses that this Lamb of God is sacrificed according to the Scripture (19:24, 28, 36–37). Worshipping God through Jesus and receiving forgiveness of sins through Jesus is not some temporary measure or a consolation prize for those who have no access to the temple. John shows that it was God's plan, right from the beginning, to replace the temple made of stone with the temple of Jesus's resurrected body (2:19–21).

Those who listen to the voice of the good shepherd and join his flock are incorporated into his body, which is a living temple. Those who worship in this temple have their sins forgiven; those who refuse to join this worship will die in their sins – just as Jesus warned (8:24).

The great authority that allowed the disciples to forgive sins – or to refuse forgiveness – was given as they were sent into the world. This empowerment was possible because of the fundamental change in their identity – the change that came through Jesus's resurrection. It was after his resurrection that Jesus called the disciples his "brothers" (20:17).

In this chapter, we will look at some aspects of John's theology of sonship: *What does it mean to be a child of God? How does this affect the disciples' attitudes towards their persecutors? And how does this help the battered disciples to recover from the shock caused by persecution?* The answers to all these questions have to do with the concept of identity; and identity, in the Fourth Gospel, is closely connected with sonship. When speaking about himself, as he often did, Jesus usually explained his identity in terms of his relationship with the Father.

In the contemporary Western world, a person's identity is often seen as a product of individual choices. In the ancient Mediterranean world, a person's identity was rooted in that of their father. As Kok explains, in ancient Mediterranean societies,

> honour was the public acknowledgement of an individual's worth by others. Should an individual be born as part of an honourable family or clan, he or she was by implication considered to be an honourable person. On the other hand, the opposite was also true. Should a person come from shameful parents, he or she was, by implication, considered to be a shameful person, seeing as his or her identity . . . was inextricably linked to the group he or she belonged to.[2]

The amount of shame or glory due to people was, to a great extent, determined by their birth. This way of thinking implies that it is impossible for people to change their identity – unless they have a new birth and new father, which is, at best, merely a hypothetical possibility. Yet, in the Gospel of John, that possibility becomes a reality.

John's first readers understood the principle of asymmetric relationship, a kind of relationship that was widespread in the Graeco-Roman world. A rich and powerful Roman patron could confer favours on his poorer or less noble

---

2. Kok, *New Perspectives*, 311.

client, in return for which the latter was expected to be grateful and loyal. The greatest possible honour was adoption, which was a widespread practice in the ancient world. A Roman could adopt an heir so that the family name would continue to exist. It went without saying that the adopted son would also do his best to increase the glory of his new family.

The more noble the adopting father, the greater the glory bestowed on the adoptee. According to the Roman way of thinking, nobody was higher than the emperor; therefore, it was hard to imagine a greater glory than being adopted by him. The Jews and proselytes believed in the living God and knew that he was infinitely higher than all earthly pagan rulers. Although God had called Israel his son (Exod 4:22), for an individual to call God his "father" would have been highly unusual.

This situation changes in the NT, where Jesus revealed God as a loving Father and made a relationship with this Father possible – through faith. When Jesus rose from the dead, he told Mary Magdalene to "go to my brothers and say to them, 'I am ascending to my Father and your Father, to my God and your God'" (John 20:17). Because of Jesus's death and resurrection, human beings are given great honour and power – "the right to become children of God . . . born, not of blood nor of the will of the flesh nor of the will of man, but of God" (1:12–13). This theme – becoming children of God through a new birth – is developed throughout the Gospel of John.

Children of God and Children of the Devil

This greatest possible honour – that of being children of God – can only be received as a gift: "A person cannot receive even one thing unless it is given him from heaven" (3:27). This humble receptive attitude of God's children is contrasted with the self-righteous disposition of some of "the Jews" who claimed the privilege of being children of Abraham and, thereby, in some way, children of God (8:39–41). But that is not who they were. Jesus boldly stated that they had no right to call Abraham their father because they were children of the devil (8:44). This verse requires a very careful approach. In the shadow of post-Holocaust Europe, such offensive language may bring to mind some displays of hatred towards the Jews that were disguised in religious terms. Some interpreters were so uncomfortable with John 8:44 and other similar verses that they preferred to explain these away by suggesting that these were not really the words of Jesus. Raymond Brown, for example, insists that it would be incredible for a twentieth-century Christian to share or to justify the Johannine contention that "the Jews" are the children of the devil, an affirmation which is *placed on the lips of Jesus* (8.44); but I cannot see how it helps contemporary Jewish-Christian relationships to disguise the fact that such an attitude once existed.[3]

In Brown's view, these words are to be understood as an emotional reaction to the expulsion from the synagogue and the accompanying trauma suffered by some of John's first readers.[4] There is, however, no need to reject the authenticity and historicity of Jesus's words in John just because evil people sometimes twist these words for their own evil purposes. As I argued in chapter 1 (see section titled "The Old Testament: A Torn Prophet for the Torn Nation"), Jesus's offensive words are to be understood in the context of the Hebrew prophetic tradition and the first-century historical situation. When properly understood in this way, it becomes obvious that those who pervert Jesus's words by using them in support of their own anti-Semitic aims do violence to those words.

When Jesus's words are properly contextualized, they become a powerful tool for Christian witness and evangelism. Jenkins describes how John 8:44 brought much encouragement to Christians in Uganda who suffered greatly under the tyrannical rule of Amin. John's gospel was one of the biblical texts that helped suffering Christians understand the spiritual, diabolical nature of Amin's regime. Raymond Brown's view of a Jesus who, allegedly, could never call anyone "children of the devil" would not be very helpful for such Christians. In fact, it would be harmful since one of the greatest spiritual needs of persecuted communities has to do with direction and boundaries – unless evil is identified and named, there is little chance of overcoming it.

Moreover, this verse can also be instrumental in leading evildoers to repentance. When removed from the context of European anti-Semitism, it can be applied to a variety of situations where evil seems to triumph, and such an application can have a powerful sobering effect. Amin was praised by propaganda and glorified as "Lord of All the Beasts of the Earth and Fishes of the Sea and Conqueror of the British Empire."[5] Now, with the benefit of

---

3. Brown, *Community*, 41–42 emphasis added.

4. As Motyer argues, this is not the only – and, perhaps, not the best – explanation of the perceived hostility towards "the Jews" in John's gospel. Motyer, *Your Father the Devil?*, 35–38.

5. The full title, according to New World Encyclopaedia, was: "His Excellency, President of Uganda, President . . . for Life, Field Marshal Al Hadji, Doctor Idi Amin, VC, Distinguished Service Order, Military Cross, Lord of All the Beasts of the Earth and Fishes of the Sea, and

hindsight, we may find these titles absurd, but for those Christians who lived and suffered under Amin's tyranny, John's gospel and the book of Revelation were sources of great encouragement that helped them see the true (demonic) character of Amin's reign.

If, for some hypothetical reason, the church in Uganda had decided to follow Raymond Brown's advice and consider John 8:44 and other similar verses as something that was "placed on the lips of Jesus," the persecuted Christians would have been deprived of an extremely important tool that helped them to perceive spiritual reality and witness to those affected by the tyranny – even the servants of the oppressive regime.

> A church leader, Kefa Sempangi, reports meeting one of Amin's Nubian assassins and torturers, who claimed to have slaughtered two hundred people. The man was converted when he read John 8:44, "Ye are of your father the devil," and he realized that in working for Amin, he had been serving Satan.[6]

Those Christian interpreters who refuse to accept John 8:44 as authentic words of Jesus may have very good intentions, but they do not help the persecuted church. In the long run, they are not merciful towards the persecutors either. The persecutors' greatest spiritual need is repentance, and it is the prophetic dimension of the gospel that may make them realize their sin, however ugly and painful that realization may be. The Fourth Evangelist shows the stark contrast between the children of God and the children of the devil. The paradox, however, is that Jesus's highly offensive remark is also a part of the good news. The children of the devil must recognize who they are, but they do not have to stay this way forever. They can become children of a different Father – through conversion and regeneration – that is, a new birth from the Spirit.

"And So We Are"

"See what kind of love the Father has given to us, that we should be called children of God; and so we are" (1 John 3:1). A Roman patrician could make legal arrangements so that his adopted son would bear his name and have the same rights and responsibilities as those of a biological son. But no human

---

Conqueror of the British Empire in Africa in General and Uganda in Particular" (https://www.newworldencyclopedia.org/entry/Idi_Amin; accessed 17/12/2023).

6. Jenkins, *New Faces*, 151; quoted in Leithart, *Revelation*, 174.

being can bridge the ontological gap between these two categories. Yet, God can do this. He does not only make "legal" arrangements for Christians to be called his children but changes who they are. He makes them "partakers of the divine nature" (2 Pet 1:4). They receive a new "spiritual DNA" – a new heart.

This change of human heart was anticipated in the OT, where Israel's many failures show that people simply cannot keep God's law. Some OT passages dealing with the restoration of Israel promise that "God will circumcise your heart" – the deep inner change that would make a person able and willing to do God's will (Deut 30:6). Prophetic denunciation of Israel's sins was accompanied by a longing for restoration.

The prophet Ezekiel, in his well-known vision of the dry bones (Ezek 37:1–14), predicts Israel's return from the Babylonian captivity. The vivid imagery of this chapter leaves no doubt that the restoration of Israel is God's work. The passage also teaches that the restoration of Israel would involve much more than simply moving a group of people from one country to another, even though this kind of migration was unheard of in the ancient world. To be fully restored, the Israelites had to experience nothing short of resurrection. In the Gospel of John, this famous passage is alluded to in a context where spiritual regeneration is discussed. But the physical, tangible character of the prophecy – which mentions bones, sinews, and skin – is also implied when Ezekiel's words are echoed in Jesus's discourse about the resurrection of the body (John 5:19–29).

God resurrects the dead, and he wanted Ezekiel to play a part in this process:

> And he said to me, "Son of man, can these bones live?" And I answered, "O LORD GOD, you know." Then he said to me, "Prophesy over these bones, and say to them, O dry bones, hear the word of the LORD. Thus says the LORD GOD to these bones: Behold, I will cause breath to enter you, and you shall live. And I will lay sinews upon you, and will cause flesh to come upon you, and cover you with skin, and put breath in you, and you shall live, and you shall know that I am the LORD." (Ezek 37:3–6)

Why was it so important for God to have the "son of man" involved in the resurrection of the dead? And who is that "son of man"? This is how God often addressed the prophet in the book of Ezekiel. In the context of that book, such an address emphasizes the frailty of human beings and, thus, their need for humility before God. The Hebrew term used (*ben-adam*) might also imply Israel's link with Adam, through whose sin all humankind fell (Rom 5:12). In the book of Daniel, however, the term "son of man" has a different meaning. In chapter 7, Daniel saw various monster-like creatures ruling over the people of God instead of being ruled by them – a situation painfully familiar to the Jews living in exile. We, too, may wonder whether humankind will ever regain dominion – the kind of power given to them at creation (Gen 1:26) – over the world. The glorious "son of man" Daniel saw is an apocalyptic figure who restores God's initial order (Dan 7:13–14).

When Jesus called himself "Son of Man" (John 1:51; 3:14; 12:23) was he emphasizing his lowliness (Phil 2:5–8) or his glorious power (as in the book of Daniel)? Or, since both aspects are paradoxically true of him, did he deliberately allow both interpretations? This view seems to tie in closely with John's understanding of Jesus's humiliation as his glorification.

In John 5:25–29 Jesus promised:

> An hour is coming, and is now here, when the dead will hear the voice of the Son of God, and those who hear will live . . . Do not marvel at this, for an hour is coming when all who are in the tombs will hear his voice and come out, those who have done good to the resurrection of life, and those who have done evil to the resurrection of judgement.

This is, of course, an allusion to Ezekiel's famous vision, with an important addition: "the son of man" is also "the Son of God." Speaking to the dead is a metaphor with a rich religious significance; but the expression also has a surprising literal meaning. In John 11, Jesus literally spoke to Lazarus, who was literally dead and literally lying in a tomb. Jesus called the dead man by his name, which, in any other circumstances, would have been a very strange thing to do. Yet, Lazarus did hear and come out (11:43–44) – as promised in John 5:28–29.

This miraculous sign may strengthen the reader's belief that Jesus, as promised in John 5:28–29, can and will cause the eschatological resurrection of the dead, which will be followed by judgement. This literal resurrection of the dead may also help us understand the metaphorical use of the images of death in the Gospel of John.

Mary Magdalene Hears His Voice

After Jesus was raised from the dead, it took his disciples some time to believe in his resurrection (John 20:9). Mary Magdalene was the first to encounter and talk to the resurrected Lord. At first, she did not believe in his resurrection; at the end of this encounter, however, she did believe and was ready to announce that good news to the disciples (20:18). When Jesus began speaking to her, she was a grieving woman, disoriented and devastated by her loss. When the conversation ended, with her being sent to do his will, she became an "apostle" to the apostles.

What caused this radical change? Seeing Jesus was, of course, part of the reason for the change in Mary; yet, seeing by itself does not automatically result in faith. Jesus spoke to her, but she did not recognize him. At some point in this conversation, she turned away from him – which was not a very polite thing to do, but a grieving woman would be free from some social conventions. She turns away from him and looks inside the grave (in the cave) – she is back to where she was before Jesus began speaking to her: "stoop[ing] to look into the tomb" (20:11). At least some part of her body seemed to have been inside the tomb so that she was, literally, one of those who were "in the tombs" (5:28) and, metaphorically, one of those "dead" who "will hear the voice of the Son of God . . . and . . . live" (5:25).

It was when Mary heard Jesus calling her by name that something changed within her. That recognition was so powerful that she became almost a different person. A few seconds before, she had not believed in his resurrection and was as good as dead herself. Now, her soul has been revived. Her spiritual renewal can be seen as anticipating both the spiritual and physical resurrection when "all who are in the tombs will hear his voice and come out" (5:28–29).[7]

Mary was restored when the "good shepherd" called her by her name. This is another promise of Jesus that came true in her life: "The sheep hear his voice, and he calls his own sheep by name and leads them out" (10:3). Jesus leads his sheep out of the place of death and hopelessness – like he did with both Lazarus and Mary Magdalene. "He goes before them, and the sheep follow him, for they know his voice" (10:4). He has gone before them through the horrific experience of death and the glorious experience of resurrection. He has also gone before them in the shameful – but also glorious – experience of being rejected by his "own nation" and its leaders (18:35).

---

7. Jesus seemed to be speaking about two resurrections – spiritual (the new birth of a believer) and physical (an eschatological event that is connected with his second coming). But he did not draw a very sharp line between these two events; thus the stories of both Lazarus (resurrected physically) and Mary Magdalene (restored spiritually) may serve as lived-out metaphors that help us understand the meaning of resurrection. Mary's experience can be seen as an example of fulfilment of both John 5:28 and John 10:3–4.

Bodies with and without Spirit

Jesus met Mary Magdalene and restored her spiritually. When she came to the disciples, they had not yet experienced that kind of restoration. Their fear and grief turned into joy (see also 16:20; 20:20) when Jesus appeared to them. With the Holy Spirit he empowered them for their apostolic ministry. The way in which the Spirit was given has a rich symbolical meaning. In Genesis 2:7, God did something similar when he created Adam. Jesus's resurrection was the beginning of the new creation. One of the first things he did after receiving back life from the Father was to give the gift of the Holy Spirit to his disciples, now called "brothers": "Jesus said to them again, 'Peace be with you. As the Father has sent me, even so I am sending you.' And when he had said this, he breathed on them and said to them, 'Receive the Holy Spirit. If you forgive the sins of any, they are forgiven them; if you withhold forgiveness from any, it is withheld'" (John 20:21–23).

This event is often called "John's Pentecost." Much has been written about how this incident relates to the Pentecost described in the book of Acts. This is not the place to discuss whether the reception of the Holy Spirit in John 20:21–23 is different from the experience described in Acts 2. What is important for our study is that the Gospel of John has a great finale, revealing the work of the Spirit. The Spirit, promised and anticipated, is here; and receiving the Spirit is closely connected with sonship, restoration, forgiveness of sins, and the disciples' mission. Now that Jesus has been raised from the dead, treating any of these themes without bringing the Spirit into the picture is inadequate. In the Gospel of John, God's great eschatological gifts – adoption by God, new birth, eternal life, the coming of the Holy Spirit, and great joy – come together. All these are inseparable from being sent into the hostile world to witness to it.

Jesus formed his disciples into a community of resurrection, forgiveness, and hope. It is impossible for this community to avoid conflict with the torn world. A disciple's proper response to the world's hostility is neither self-isolation nor compromising with the world's values but, rather, courageous witness. These two communities have different values because their members have different identities: different fathers, different spiritual origins, and different prospects for the future. The lines between the two communities will be drawn, but they will sometimes be drawn in an unpredictable manner. In the following section, we will look at both separation and crossing the boundaries, using the example of Nicodemus, one of the most controversial characters in the Fourth Gospel. As we look at Nicodemus – his initial failure to understand the truth about new birth and his eventual transformation – I will try to show how a prophecy from the book of Ezekiel forms the background for understanding some of the truths ironically revealed through this torn man's participation in the gospel story.

The Parting of the Ways: The Case of Nicodemus
A Failed Teacher

When the prophet Ezekiel obeyed God's command, dead bones turned into living bodies. God demonstrated his power by creating living human beings from these bones. Of course, he could have created people without using those old bones, but, for Ezekiel's theology, it was important to emphasize continuity in God's dealing with Israel. The use of the bones implies that God does not create completely new human beings but, rather, restores life to those who lived and died some time ago. In Babylonian captivity, Israel was restored through repentance and became a renewed nation. But it was still Israel – and not some other ethnic group – that came back to the promised land.

Sin – and the death that results from it – represents the worst kind of discontinuity, but God's power is great enough to provide continuity even when, humanly speaking, none is possible. Some discontinuity, however, remains. Ezekiel draws the reader's attention to the fact that the restoration of the dead nation would occur in two stages.

> So I prophesied as I was commanded. And as I prophesied, there was a sound, and behold, a rattling, and the bones came together, bone to its bone. And I looked, and behold, there were sinews on them, and flesh had come upon them, and skin had covered them. But there was no breath in them. (Ezek 37:7–8)

The lifeless bodies were already here. But there was still no life-giving breath in them. The breath would come soon, but Ezekiel wanted the reader to stop and take in this moment. This is similar to the creation of Adam, where, when the body of the first man was formed, he did not become a living creature until God breathed life into him (Gen 2:7).[8]

Ezekiel's visual metaphor is applicable to postexilic Israel. The nation returned from Babylon, but it had not yet been fully restored. Israel was still a torn people. Obviously, political independence and monarchy were absent, but something else was missing too. Expectation of God's intervention was

---

8. In John 20, the disciples were also far from experiencing the promised abundance of life – until Jesus breathed the Spirit into them.

very high. In John's gospel, one of the aspects of this expected intervention has to do with God's Spirit.

It has become common in biblical interpretation to assert that the Jews of Jesus's day were hoping for a military liberation from Rome, whereas Jesus brought spiritual blessings, in which they were not so interested. But there is no need to overemphasize this distinction. In the OT, when God's Spirit came upon an individual, it often resulted in the person being empowered for physical combat. Jephthah (Judg 11:29), Samson (15:14), Saul (1 Sam 11:6), David (1 Sam 16:13), and other leaders of God's people were able to physically defeat their enemies because God's Spirit was upon them.[9]

Jesus announced the coming outpouring of God's Spirit – something that was greatly desired but often misunderstood. John indicates that the leaders of Israel were to blame for much of that misunderstanding. The example of Nicodemus – "the teacher of Israel" (John 3:10) who came to Jesus at night (3:2) – is one of the stories John uses to emphasize this point.

Jesus spoke to Nicodemus about the cleansing that comes through water, about restoration and regeneration that are tantamount to being raised from the dead, and about experiencing a new birth. Ezekiel 36–37 is a long and well-known OT passage where these three themes are discussed at length and illustrated by powerful imagery. Jesus made several allusions to this passage, but Nicodemus failed to grasp these. These allusions are not particularly easy to detect since Ezekiel uses the same Hebrew word for "wind" and "spirit," and Jesus did the same in Greek. One could sympathize with Nicodemus if it were not that he was an established interpreter of the OT – "the teacher of Israel." In Keener's opinion,

> especially after the connection between the Spirit and water (3:5), the informed reader will likely recognize "wind" as a metaphor for God's life-giving Spirit (esp. Ezek 37:9–14, which follows naturally after the allusion to Ezek 36 in John 3:5), an image further reinforced by the Gospel's climactic pneumatological passage (20:22).[10]

Nicodemus could not understand Jesus's teaching about new birth from the Spirit because this teaching is based on the OT, and, according to John,

---

9. And when God withdrew his Spirit from Saul (1 Sam 16:14), courage and wisdom were also gone from him, as evident in the story of Goliath and some other passages.

10. Keener, *Commentary*, 557.

Nicodemus did not have an adequate understanding of the OT.[11] And it is not just that Nicodemus happened to hold to a different interpretation of some prophecies; it is worse – he failed as an interpreter because he was unable to even catch the allusions to these well-known passages.

Jesus was known to show mercy to people whose human dignity had been nearly destroyed by sin – and sometimes religion, too. He described himself as "gentle and lowly in heart" (Matt 11:29). His very first miracle reported in John was done in order to save people from shame (John 2:3). But Jesus responded differently to Nicodemus and many other Jewish leaders. Jesus put Nicodemus to shame by deliberately highlighting the discrepancy between Nicodemus's high status – exaggerated to make the putdown even more embarrassing[12] – and his failure to act in accordance with this status. Why did Jesus do this?

Before answering this question, it is helpful to look at a passage found towards the end of the Gospel of John, where we see Nicodemus helping to bury Jesus (19:39–40). Apparently, this experience of being shamed did not make Nicodemus turn away from Jesus. Nicodemus demonstrated remarkable loyalty at a time when even Jesus's own (male) disciples failed to do so. This member of the Sanhedrin publicly identified with Jesus when very few were brave enough to do so. Jesus knew that this act of shaming to which he subjected Nicodemus would not destroy their relationship. To be precise, Jesus did destroy the relationship Nicodemus was trying to have with him but graciously offered him a relationship of a different kind, a relationship that held the promise of salvation. This description may sound complicated because it describes complex aspects of social and spiritual reality. But let us try to untangle the complexity in two steps.

"We-You": A Relationship Destroyed

In most modern editions of the Bible, the passage in which Jesus converses with Nicodemus begins at John 3:1. That chapter division is unfortunate because the last verse(s) of chapter 2 forms an insightful introduction to that conversation. Two important truths must be kept in mind as we approach the passage. First,

---

11. As I argue in chapter 4 (see section titled "The Disciples as a Group"), Jesus gave his disciples a new understanding of the OT as a whole, not just an explanation of separate passages.

12. The (definite) article used here – "the teacher of Israel" – strengthens Jesus's sarcastic question. Nicodemus was, of course, just one of the many teachers of the law, so, strictly speaking, he was "*a* teacher of Israel"; but, in their discussion, Jesus deliberately exaggerated Nicodemus's status and contrasted this with his helplessness. This is shaming: Nicodemus was made aware of the fact that his skills did not match his role and status.

Jesus knew everything there was to know about his conversation partner: "for he himself knew what was in man [a form of the noun ἄνθρωπος, *anthropos*]" (2:25). Second, Nicodemus is described as a "man [ἄνθρωπος, *anthropos*]" (3:1). Perhaps there is a third clue as well: Jesus is "the true light, which enlightens everyone [πάντα ἄνθρωπον, *panta anthropon*]" (1:9), and Nicodemus came by night[13] to meet the "true light." His encounter with the "light" would be painful and like nothing he could have anticipated.

Nicodemus seemed to come to Jesus alone;[14] yet, when speaking to Jesus, he used the pronoun "we," which could sound as if he were speaking on behalf of some unspecified group of people. Perhaps he was trying to make his position seem stronger than it really was. But Nicodemus also came to Jesus as a human being (ἄνθρωπος, *anthropos*) in need of salvation. Nicodemus was a torn man, who remained torn for much of the rest of John's gospel; but Jesus changed the way in which he was torn so that Nicodemus could achieve wholeness.

There are two aspects to the way Jesus dealt with Nicodemus. Nicodemus was rejected as a member of a powerful group but accepted as a human being without any special status. It is not easy to describe this pattern in modern English, but a schematic description could look like this: Jesus rejected the "we-you" relationship that Nicodemus tried to impose on him[15] and offered Nicodemus a saving "I-Thou" relationship instead.

When Nicodemus called Jesus "Rabbi," this address implied a certain set of expectations. Nicodemus's view of Jesus was too low. In a condescending sort of way, Nicodemus indicated that there was social distance between them but that he was willing to decrease this distance and treat Jesus as a fellow teacher. The truth is that the distance between them was enormous – it was the distance between the holy Son of God and a sinful man. But, in his great humility, Jesus stepped into the situation created by Nicodemus's false expectations. He

---

13. Of course, there might have been any number of reasons Nicodemus chose to come to Jesus in the (literal) night-time. Yet, the passage is loaded with symbolism that becomes especially prominent by contrast with John 13:30, where Judas walked away into the night. Two opposite directions are present here: towards the light and away from the light. This is, of course, greatly simplified because even for those people who are drawn to the light, there is not always steady progress and they tend to go back and forth. Their encounters with the light may be traumatic, healing, or puzzling. But, in the long run, all people either move towards the light or away from it.

14. Some commentators find it unthinkable that a person of such high status would walk around Jerusalem by himself. But to assume that Nicodemus did not come alone seems to read into the text something that does not go well with the singular form of the verb "came" (John 3:2).

15. Note the plural "we" and the plural "you" (harder to identify in English) in John 3:11.

responded as a teacher and, as a teacher, showed that Nicodemus had no right to treat him in this manner.

Of course, not all commentators share this view. Some even see Jesus's conversation with Nicodemus as some kind of "failure." Neyrey's opinion is remarkably pessimistic: "Teachers teach, but when Jesus tries to teach Nicodemus, he utterly fails. Does this reflect on the teacher or the pupil? Jesus continues speaking to Nicodemus, but without results."[16] I disagree with Neyrey's conclusion because I cannot agree with his premise. Teachers do not only teach; Jewish teachers of the law also engaged each other in debates about interpretations of the law. This is exactly what Jesus did here. He started a discussion about the OT and then showed that Nicodemus was not qualified to discuss this matter with him.

Nicodemus offered Jesus the possibility of a relationship where Jesus would be treated as a gifted junior partner. Jesus ruined that possibility, and he did so in a way that must have hurt Nicodemus – by attacking his professional competence. Nicodemus was drawn to the light, and the exposure to the light resulted in shame. In this light, Nicodemus's inadequacy became visible. Exposure to light entails judgement.

How would Nicodemus respond? Many characters in the Gospel of John turned away from the light. Since they belonged to the torn world, they did what the world does. Some crawled back into the darkness trying to escape judgement – and by doing so, brought judgement on themselves. Others attacked both the light and the disciples who were bearers of this light and, by so doing, made their guilt even greater. But Nicodemus seemed to stay, even though the experience was far from pleasant.

"I-Thou": A New Relationship Offered

When Nicodemus stopped arguing, Jesus offered him an interpretation of another OT passage – the story of the bronze serpent (Num 21:6–9). This allusion is easier to grasp, but Nicodemus's role had changed. Since he could contribute little to the discussion, it seemed best for him to listen – as a pupil and not as a teacher. After he was put to shame (John 3:10), the dialogue became a monologue by Jesus. But as Nicodemus listened, the possibility of a new relationship opened up to him – a relationship through faith: "And as Moses lifted up the serpent in the wilderness, so must the Son of Man be lifted up, that whoever believes in him may have eternal life" (3:14–15).

---

16. Neyrey, *Gospel of John*, 76.

Nicodemus could receive this eternal life, but he could only do so as a human being (ἄνθρωπος, *anthropos*) for whom Christ died. A high social status does not confer any benefits in this respect and can even make the situation more difficult by creating false expectations. Jesus rejected a "we-you" relationship with the (invisible) group of people Nicodemus sought to represent and then graciously opened up the possibility of a faith-based, saving personal ("I-Thou") relationship with him.

As Köstenberger notes,

> Jesus' assertive stance toward Nicodemus strikingly demonstrates for John's readers that Jesus, while falling short of Nicodemus' rabbinic credentials, commanded spiritual authority far exceeding that of his Jewish counterpart. It was doubtless impressive to many of John's original readers that later in the Gospel Nicodemus ends up a secret follower of Jesus.[17]

To take this observation one step further, Jesus was assertive towards an authority figure but gracious towards a human being. In his great wisdom, he knows how to address the enormously complex experience of a torn individual in a torn world.

Nicodemus appears in the Gospel of John three times and, in each instance, is portrayed as suffering a great deal of shame. As explained above, he was shamed by Jesus (3:10). Next, he is shown participating in a council meeting where many expressed their contempt towards Jesus. When Nicodemus tried to protest, his colleagues snubbed him in a rather boorish way: "Are you from Galilee too? Search and see that no prophet arises from Galilee" (7:52). This kind of attitude involves manipulating with shame. The other members of the Sanhedrin pretended to question Nicodemus's origin, associating him with Galilee – a region whose inhabitants they deeply despised and described in crude stereotypes. They indicated that Nicodemus's behaviour was not in line with the values of this group that he belonged to.

Nicodemus tried to have a discussion about the law and the proper legal procedures: "Does our law judge a man without first giving him a hearing and learning what he does?" (7:51). But it turns out that his conversation partners did not qualify for such a discussion. As Jesus had earlier explained, they studied the law in order to gain glory for themselves (5:44). This was not the kind of setting where an objective discussion of Jesus's actions and the corresponding OT passage was likely to take place.

---

17. Köstenberger, "Jesus as Rabbi," 109.

Nicodemus's opponents added another insult, which implied that he had limited knowledge of the Scriptures (7:52). Their suggestion that he "search" means "search the Scriptures." Nicodemus's question was dealt with in a patronizing kind of way, which was another widespread shaming technique – treating the person as if he were someone with limited experience or intelligence.[18]

Jesus shamed Nicodemus for his inadequate knowledge of Scripture. The other Pharisees also shamed Nicodemus for his allegedly poor knowledge of Scripture. There is, however, a world of difference between these two experiences of being shamed. Jesus put Nicodemus through the unpleasant experience of being shamed in order to make him wiser and destroy the false identity that Nicodemus was trying to build. The Pharisees shamed Nicodemus in order to avoid an honest discussion and protect the false identities they had been building.

The third time Nicodemus appears in the Gospel of John, he identified with Jesus by helping to bury him. Doing so would have made him an object of much scorn since he could expect to experience some of the shame that the world poured upon Jesus on the cross. Had Nicodemus finally understood the meaning of the passage describing the bronze serpent? Would he experience new birth from the Spirit? These are open questions; it is hard to say how far Nicodemus had come in his relationship with Jesus. However, we do see him move in the right direction.

Nicodemus's story seems to be related to a question that is often discussed by interpreters of the Fourth Gospel: What is John's attitude towards secret disciples? On the one hand, John criticizes those who were afraid to confess their faith in Jesus, stating that "they loved the glory that comes from man more than the glory that comes from God" (12:43). On the other hand, even characters in his gospel who believed in Jesus are hardly ever portrayed as exhibiting a strong, mature faith right from the beginning. Their faith is not static but grows as it struggles and overcomes one crisis after another. So, it may be reasonable to keep one's faith secret while it is still weak. Secret disciples, such as Joseph of Arimathea, do exist. Joseph is not called a false disciple or an apostate, and his discipleship is real, although, of course, greatly limited.

---

18. Ironically, if Nicodemus and his colleagues had really done a comprehensive Bible study on "prophets from Galilee," the result would have surprised them. They would have discovered that the prophet Jonah came from Gath-hepher (2 Kgs 14:25; Josh 19:13). Another layer of John's irony is evident in the fact that after the catastrophe of AD 70, Galilee became home base for teachers of the law (many of whom had fled from Judea).

But John shows that "secret discipleship" is not meant to be a permanent state. Sooner or later, a secret disciple must give glory to God by witnessing to Jesus. When does the moment come when keeping one's faith a secret is not an option any more? Each individual case is, of course, unique; and much depends on how dangerous it would be to confess the faith that is not welcome in the group one tries to hide it from. It is clear, though, that when a group actively persecutes Christ – by persecuting Christians – failure to confess Christ would mean tacit support for the persecution.[19]

A torn person will be shamed – either by Jesus or by the world or, as Nicodemus's experience shows, by both – until a firm decision is made to be loyal to one of the two masters. Shaming means a crisis in the relationship. It is expected that those who are shamed will change their attitudes and behaviour since these do not correspond to the values of the group. If they yield to this pressure, the relationship may continue and even become stronger. If they refuse, more shame may be applied – until the relationship is destroyed.

The world uses shaming techniques to put pressure on the followers of Christ. But Christ also shames the world. He did this, above all, by being raised from the dead. In resurrecting Christ, the Father gave him great glory, which automatically means great shame and dishonour for those who fail to honour Christ. The only way to avoid "shame and everlasting contempt" (Dan 12:2) is to share in the shame of Jesus and his persecuted community – that is, the church.

Summary

This chapter has discussed how God deals with torn people who have suffered – or are about to suffer – rejection from their "own." God acts in a paradoxical way. Believers become his children through faith and spiritual regeneration – that is, new birth – but, after experiencing this new birth, they do not cease to be torn individuals. In fact, their condition often gets worse: their conflict with mainstream Judaism – and, in the contemporary world, with many other groups that do not accept Jesus as the Son of God – becomes bitter and reaches a breaking point.

The Gospel of John strengthens such Christians in many ways. First, it deepens their awareness of who they are in Christ – children of God. In the world, where an individual's identity cannot be separated from that of their

---

19. This is, of course, just a general observation, to which there are many exceptions such as the example of Obadiah (1 Kgs 18:3–16).

biological or adoptive father, John shows that the only way to avoid a shameful identity is to be adopted by God through the resurrected Christ. This adoption changes everything, but God does not stop at merely declaring that believers are his children. He also produces within them an internal change that is so profound that it can be called a spiritual resurrection. This spiritual resurrection is closely connected with and anticipates our physical resurrection. We saw in Ezekiel's prophecy, in which dead bones come to life, that there is a complex interplay between the physical and spiritual aspects of that resurrection.

In Ezekiel's vision, physical resurrection took place first, followed by a spiritual resurrection. In the experience of many followers of Christ, this sequence is reversed. In John 20, Mary Magdalene and the other disciples first experienced spiritual restoration, and that experience then became for them another confirmation that their physical (eschatological) resurrection was coming. This same order can also be traced in the lives of modern Christians: their spiritual regeneration – their new birth – makes them look forward to the eschatological resurrection of their bodies.

Being a community of resurrection, the disciples – that is, God's children – would not be able to avoid further conflict with mainstream Judaism. Their persecutors were children of a different father; and since they refused to have their sins forgiven, they would have a different destiny. At some point, the lines between the two communities would have to be drawn.

While it may sound very harsh for Jesus to refer to his persecutors as children of the devil, in a paradoxical kind of way, this sharp redrawing of the boundaries allows the children of the devil to convert and become children of God, thereby escaping shame and destruction.

The parting of the ways is accompanied by the experience of intense shame. The two groups separating from each other have different fathers and, therefore, different values and different systems of reward and punishment. We have already considered how Nicodemus experienced shame three times in the Gospel of John and how those experiences changed him.

In the beginning, Nicodemus wanted to have a "we-you" relationship with Jesus, trying to gain his favour by claiming membership in some influential group. Jesus showed him the futility of such an attempt. There is only one way to be saved – through a personal ("I-Thou") relationship with Jesus, a relationship that is not based on any human merit but solely on God's grace. It is in the context of such a relationship that a new birth – with all its associated benefits such as the forgiveness of sins, the gift of the Holy Spirit, eternal life, and the anticipation of a glorious physical resurrection – is possible.

In this chapter, I have dealt with the questions "Who are we?" and "Where are we from?" In the next chapter, I will discuss an answer to the third fundamental question of human existence: "Where are we going?"

3

Where Are We Going?

What is the purpose of our existence? Many answers have been offered to this age-old question, but few are as profound or as concise as the one given at the beginning of the Westminster Shorter Catechism: "Man's chief end is to glorify God and to enjoy him forever." Most Christians would agree with this statement – at least to some extent – but what exactly does it mean to glorify God? As we saw in the previous chapter, one person's glory can be another's shame. In this chapter, we will look at how Jesus glorified the Father, and this will help us answer some of the questions related to the destiny of torn disciples.

God does everything for his glory, and he is perfectly righteous in doing so. Unfortunately, fallen human beings want to be like God and try to glorify themselves, which results in sin. The torn world does not seek to glorify God (thus rejecting the purpose of its own existence) but glories in itself. The good news is that God is going to put an end to this and bring the world to a state in which "the earth will be filled with the knowledge of the glory of the LORD as the waters cover the sea" (Hab 2:14). In fact, with the first coming of Christ, God had already begun changing the world.

The persecuted community of torn disciples was promised God's eternal glory (John 17:22, 24). This was their future, and this anticipated future had already begun to shape their present experience. They could already see God's glory in the present, in their suffering. How were they able to do this?

The Story of the Blind Man
Thrown Out of the Synagogue

The gospels are books about Jesus, and he is the main character in nearly every narrative. One of the very few exceptions is John 9, where Jesus appears and acts at the beginning and end of the chapter (9:1–7, 35–41) but is absent for twenty-seven verses in the middle (9:8–34). This is the longest gospel passage with Jesus absent.[1]

The blind man, though healed, had not seen Jesus yet.[2] He had heard Jesus, experienced his touch and the application of his saliva, and would, eventually, see him. But before he saw his Saviour, the blind man had to undergo a trial. As a result of his courageous testimony, the blind man would be kicked out of the synagogue. And after that – and *only after* that – will he see Jesus.

The blind man's experience was obviously important for John, who describes this man's trials in great detail. Louis J. Martyn makes some crucial observations about the similarities between the story of Jesus, the story of the blind man, and the story of the persecuted community for whom the Fourth Gospel was written. The blind man, like Jesus and his first-century followers, was attacked and rejected by the religious authorities. Like Jesus, the blind man stood firm and testified to the truth.

According to Martyn, this episode contains a paradigm for the story of Christian conversion in the persecuted community. Someone hears words of Christ (spoken through a preacher), experiences a new birth, a spiritual opening of their eyes. They begin to see things in a very different light, and then the conflict with mainstream Judaism begins. Martyn's method is called "two-level hermeneutic." On one level, the Gospel can be read as a story of Jesus; on another level, it can be read as a story of a persecuted community. This approach, developed in the 1960s, became highly influential in Johannine studies. Even those scholars who were extremely sceptical about the two-level hermeneutic could not afford to ignore it altogether. I, too, will use this approach here, although with some serious reservations.[3]

---

1. This is true if we do not count the passages in Matthew and Luke that tell us about Jesus's genealogy and the events preceding his birth. But those passages describe what happens before Jesus appears, not after he disappears (like in 9:8–34).

2. As I argue in chapter 4 (see section titled "Already, but Not Yet"), this liminal state, "already, but not yet," can be discerned in the lives of both the gospel characters and modern readers.

3. Those reservations are many; here, I note just two of them. First, Martyn rejects (rather offhandedly) the possibility of the apostolic origin of the Fourth Gospel. If a book that places so much emphasis on the theme of testimony was not written by an eyewitness (John 19:35), then there is a serious ethical problem undermining its credibility. Second, Martyn believes that separation between the church and the synagogue began after changes in the synagogal liturgy that were introduced by the Council of Jamnia. According to Martyn's reconstruction, at some point at the end of the first century, the prayer called "Eighteen Benedictions" was supplemented with *Birkat ha-Minim* – the so-called "benediction" (a euphemism for "cursing") of heretics, which included Christians (*notzrim*). Those Jews who believed in Jesus could no

Giving Glory to God

> So for the second time they called the man who had been blind and said to him, "Give glory to God. We know that this man is a sinner." (John 9:24)

This is another instance where John's irony is manifested in a powerful way. The former blind man was summoned by the Pharisees again; but this time, there is some semblance of legal procedure involved. The accusers, who also functioned as judges, demanded that the former blind man make an official statement of sorts – the equivalent of speaking under oath in a contemporary legal system. They used an expression originally borrowed from Joshua 7:19: "Then Joshua said to Achan, 'My son, give glory to the LORD God of Israel and give praise to him. And tell me now what you have done; do not hide it from me.'" This is a very interesting expression, so it may be helpful to look at what it meant in the original OT context and what two meanings are implied in the context of the gospel story.

In the book of Joshua, the conversation referred to took place after Israel's defeat at Ai. God refused to help the Israelites in their fight and then explained the reason for his refusal: one of the warriors had broken his commandment. God even indicated who that warrior was. Achan, the culprit, was singled out. If Achan admitted his guilt, God's ways would be justified in the eyes of all Israel, and it would be made known to everyone that God – unlike the capricious deities of Israel's neighbours – is faithful to his word. God always acts in accordance with his holy nature and does everything for his glory.

If Achan's guilt was confirmed, God would have been glorified, and it would have been obvious that God's righteousness was beyond all reproach. If Achan denied his guilt, this would have created a false impression that God had withdrawn his promised military help without good reason. "If we confess our sins, he is faithful and just to forgive us our sins and to cleanse us from all unrighteousness. If we say we have not sinned, we make him a liar, and his word is not in us" (1 John 1:9–10). Achan confessed his guilt because he was confronted with God's omniscience, and this became an important lesson for Israel. God knows all our secrets (Matt 6:4, 6, 18; John 2:24–25). When we speak the truth, even if that truth is unpleasant, we bring glory to God.

---

longer participate in such worship since this would involve invoking curses on themselves. While Martyn's hypothesis is fascinating, it is based on an assumption rather than on solid historical facts. As Köstenberger points out, one indisputable fact – the destruction of Jerusalem – receives far less attention in Martyn's work than it deserves. Köstenberger, "Destruction," 218.

A millennium and a half later, the same expression was used in a different context and with a radically different intention. It is possible that the phrase itself had become an idiom or a legal formula of sorts.[4] In John 9, we read how this formula was used in a manipulative, dishonest way that breaks the third of the Ten Commandments. The Pharisees put pressure on the former blind man, trying to make him slander Jesus. By refusing to submit to them and accept their twisted version of what had happened in his own life, the man gave glory to God – which, if the Pharisees' request is taken literally, was exactly what they had asked him to do. John skilfully plays on the differences and similarities between the literal and idiomatic meanings of the phrase "give glory to God," strengthening the connection between a Christian's courageous testimony and God's glory.

This connection is an extremely important motivating factor for followers of Jesus in every age. We can ask ourselves, "Why does God want us to witness?" This is not a rhetorical question. As we reflect on possible answers, our reflection may reveal a lot about our theology of witness. For some believers, the main driving force is "winning people for Christ." And indeed, seeing people convert to Christianity brings great joy. Yet, according to John, this should not be our chief motivation. The blind man bore witness to Jesus – wisely and bravely – but he did not "win" anyone in his audience to Christ. Jesus himself witnessed to the truth as he stood before Pilate (18:37), but he did not "win" Pilate. Nor did he "win" the crowd or the disciples who turned away from him after his "bread of life" discourse (6:66). Jesus witnessed to the truth because that is why he came to the world. We are to bear witness to the truth because we are also sent into the world. As we bear witness to the truth, we give glory to God – and that must be our ultimate motivation.

John's irony is evident throughout this passage. The former blind man – who had no education and no social status – put to shame the Pharisees and theologians because he glorified God, whereas his opponents sought to glorify themselves.

Being thrown out of the synagogue would not have been a pleasant experience for anyone. For this former blind man, it was a personal disaster. He had been totally dependent on other people; now, all the significant others in his social world had rejected him. Even his own parents refused to stand up for him (9:18–23). He had no income, no skills – except for some begging

---

4. Just as in the United States, for example, a sworn witness may be officially asked, "Do you solemnly swear that you will tell the truth, the whole truth, and nothing but the truth, so help you God?"

techniques – and now that he was no longer blind, he probably could not beg either. Earlier, he had not had much; but now, he had lost everything. In that moment, he was a complete nobody. His previous life was over, and the door to the past had been slammed shut. It is in this condition of "social death" that Jesus met him (9:35). We are not told what happened after the man worshipped Jesus, but one thing is clear – a whole new life had begun for him.

This is Jesus's great gift to his followers – a new life, which presupposes a new birth. This new life comes with trials but also with many of God's blessings. One of these blessings is the ability to "see" – a unique spiritual perception of things that is given to God's children. John, in many passages of his gospel, seems to encourage his readers to practise this ability, which could lead to some unexpected discoveries. Discipleship results in a radical change of one's worldview – that is, a very different way of seeing the world and one's place in it.

Jesus's disciples and their persecutors might have looked at the same events happening in their shared social space, but their interpretations of those events was sometimes radically different. The most important of such events was, of course, Jesus's crucifixion.

Jesus's Death: Not a Tragedy

Most people in this world are familiar with the fact that Jesus was crucified, but relatively few understand the meaning of that event. Jesus is often seen as a good man who happened to fall into the hands of bad rulers; and evil, unfortunately, triumphed – as it still sometimes does in our day. This interpretation, popular both in secular and religious circles, makes one able to sympathize with Jesus without being transformed by the power of his death and resurrection. This interpretation may seem comforting; from time to time, we all experience injustice, and since Jesus seems to be "one of us" – another innocent person suffering – we may feel less lonely. In some of our worst moments, we do experience a terrible feeling of loneliness and helplessness, where our lives spin out of control and circumstances we could not even imagine seem to crush us completely. We may feel like helpless victims, broken toys in the hands of a cruel child who is bent on meaningless destruction.

Crucifixion may seem like the worst form of helplessness. The condemned person lost all control of his arms and legs, and he had no control over the extent of his exposure to the ridicule of the crowd. The excruciating pain would make any kind of calm and composure impossible. It was more than just torture and slow death – a person's very identity was being obliterated.

Ancient readers would have a category that could help them understand the horror of crucifixion. They knew what tragedy was. The hero (or the heroine) driven by some noble desires falls into a trap – in a situation where some forces beyond his control ruin his life. Here it may be helpful to look at a tragedy – as a literary genre and a broader category for interpreting real events.

Tragic Heroes in the Old Testament

Since pious Jews in Jesus's day usually despised Greek theatre, they would not have used the word "tragedy" to describe events taking place in their own cultural context. Yet, they understood the *concept* of tragedy quite well. The OT Scriptures that formed their thinking were full of tragic heroes and heroines – tragic in the literal (or rather, literary-critical) meaning of that word. Take, for example, Tamar, David's daughter, who was raped by her half-brother. This was a tragic event that ruined her life, and what made it even more tragic is that she became a victim of that crime because she had obeyed her father's orders. Since the readers of the book of Samuel already know about Amnon and Jonadab's evil plan (2 Sam 13:3–5), they can see how King David was manipulated into unwittingly participating in that plan. Obedience to a king and father is normally a good thing but, for Tamar, it had disastrous consequences. That is tragedy at its clearest expression – a virtuous virgin became a helpless victim of the evil powers that overwhelmed her.

> In hiding places [the wicked] murders the innocent.
>   His eyes stealthily watch for the helpless;
> he lurks in ambush like a lion in his thicket;
>   he lurks that he may seize the poor;
> he seizes the poor when he draws him into his net.
> The helpless are crushed, sink down, and fall by his might.
>   (Ps 10:8–10)

Tamar's brother Absalom is another tragic character, although of a different kind. He tried to act as a hero, driven by noble motives – to restore justice and to protect his sister's good name (or what was left of it). At first, there seems to be nothing victim-like about Absalom. Yet, in the end, he also fell prey to evil, and much of that evil resided in his own heart. His tragic story has many *if onlys*. *If only* David had done what the king was supposed to do and punished the evildoer . . . *If only* David had not been so harsh with Absalom and forgave him fully . . . As in a classic Greek tragedy, Absalom tried to avoid what he saw as evil; and the more he tried, the more entangled he became in evil schemes. At the end of the story, when he hung on a tree-branch caught by his hair (2 Sam 18:9), that entanglement became literal. Although Absalom had not planned this outcome, it was brought about largely through his own decisions. The more he tried to control the adverse circumstances, the less power he had over them.

Both the OT and the NT have many more examples of tragic characters and situations. In the Gospel of John, for example, the Jewish leaders, selfish as they were, fit the pattern of tragic characters in many ways. The chief priests and the Pharisees were afraid that the Romans would destroy them: "and the Romans will come and take away both our place [the Temple] and our nation" (John 11:48). The Romans did come in AD 70, and they did "take away" the holy place. Since we know that this happened because the religious leaders persecuted Jesus and the early church,[5] we can see how the Pharisees took one step after another towards the destruction of Jerusalem – the very thing they had hoped to avoid.

Rejecting "If Onlys"

The Bible realistically describes the plight of living in a fallen world, and modern readers can also identify with such descriptions. When we read in the news about children killed in air strikes in Ukraine, we call it a tragedy, and rightly so. Those children could have been growing up and enjoying a normal life instead of facing a senseless death. We can easily imagine an alternative scenario: what it would be like if only there was no war.

Tragedy always presupposes an alternative scenario that could have been realized if only the tragic element – the invasion of evil – had not happened. Romeo and Juliet could have lived happily ever after if only the messenger had not been delayed. Hamlet could have killed the wicked Claudius and become king if only he had not lingered at the moment when Claudius was in his power. We can easily identify with such situations because we see them – hopefully, on a smaller scale – in our own lives. A tragedy always implies that there is an alternative "happy ending" and that the "if only" event triggered the worst-case scenario.

In Jesus's case, it seems easy enough to imagine what his life would have been like if it had not been destroyed by the cross. So many more people could have been healed and taught, humankind could have enjoyed so many more

---

5. Passages such as Luke 21:20–22 do not leave much doubt as to what the Synoptics believed to be the main reason for the tragedy of AD 70.

benefits – if only. If only Judas or Pilate or the high priests or the ignorant crowds had not been so successful in their evil plans. It is natural to see the cross as interrupting and destroying God's great gift to the world, which is how Peter once saw it (Matt 16:22).

It is remarkable that Jesus himself completely rejected that kind of interpretation of his death (Matt 16:23). He insisted that it was his own decision to go to the cross and that no one had forced him to do so: "I lay down my life that I may take it up again. No one takes it from me, but I lay it down of my own accord. I have authority to lay it down, and I have authority to take it up again" (John 10:17–18). Judas's betrayal was not an "if only" event that thwarted some good plan. Jesus knew that this would happen; and, on the night he was betrayed, he even initiated the series of events that he knew would make Judas's wicked heart respond exactly the way it did.[6]

Pilate hesitated to sentence Jesus to death – and we might think that this is another "if only" event. If only Pilate had decided not to let the high priests manipulate him . . . If only he had not felt the need to please them at that moment . . . If only the crowd had chosen Jesus instead of Barabbas . . . The passion story is full of such moments upon which Jesus's fate seemed to hinge. Yet, Jesus refused to see things this way. He had already accepted the cross, and he did not try to escape it. This is why he was so assertive with Judas, the high priest, Pilate, and all the other people who thought they had power over him.

It was Jesus's decision to lay down his life; and as he acted upon this decision, no one could stand in his way. When Pilate contemplated setting Jesus free, without knowing it, he was thinking about opposing God's plan. Jesus carried out what he had decided to do not just in spite of Pilate's weakness, but through Pilate's weakness and lack of discernment. The Gospel of John portrays Jesus as being in control of all that happened during his passion, from beginning to end.

Glory as the Opposite of Tragedy

After his arrest, Jesus was treated in a most cruel and humiliating way. Yet, he was never a helpless victim. The Synoptic Gospels show that he was repeatedly tortured and shamed. But, on the third day, God resurrected him. This resurrection reverses everything. The glory of the resurrected Christ can be seen as God's recompense for all the shame Jesus suffered. One can see a symbolic V-shaped motion in his life: he keeps going down into the depths

---

6. See John 6:70–71.

of suffering and humiliation, but after he reaches the lowest point, his ascent to glory begins.

This is how the Synoptics viewed Jesus's suffering and glory. The apostle Paul seemed to have had similar views.[7] He writes about the Son of God going down from heavenly glory to being a man and then the downward vertical motion continuing with Jesus assuming the role of a slave – a person with the lowest social status. Then, Jesus accepted death, which also implies a downward motion – from the world of the living to the realm of the dead. But even that is not the lowest point for not all kinds of death are the same – and death by crucifixion was, by far, the worst. The descent from heavenly glory to death on the cross covers the longest possible symbolic vertical distance. There is no higher point from which one could start. There is no lower point that could be reached on the descent.

Then God changed everything and, from that depth of total dishonour, lifted Jesus to God's glory again. Paul teaches his readers to discern the same pattern in their own lives. Being a Christian in the first-century Roman Empire often meant persecution accompanied by decrease in one's social status. This symbolic downward motion has both social and physical (and quite literal) aspects. At the end of our earthly lives, our bodies are usually lowered into the grave. This is not what we were originally created for, and this may be one of the reasons Paul wrote about our "lowly [ταπεινώσεως, *tapeinoseos*] body" (Phil 3:21). Adam and Eve were created to rule over the earth on God's behalf. For God's viceroys and their children, it is humiliating to decompose in the earth instead of ruling over it.

Paul was strengthening the Philippians' hope of their own resurrection – the moment when God would reward them for all they had lost in this life. The same V-shaped pattern would also be discernible in their lives stretching far beyond the grave. The apostle Peter teaches a similar lesson: "Humble yourselves, therefore, under the mighty hand of God so that at the proper time he may exalt you" (1 Pet 5:6). Similar instructions can be found in the Epistle of James (4:10) and many other NT texts.

This movement – from dishonour to glory – does not fit into the paradigm of tragedy. The ancient readers had a different category for understanding this

---

7. Philippians 2:6–10.

pattern – namely, a story of glorification.[8] In the following paragraphs, we will take a brief look at some parallels in the OT and the ancient world.

Old Testament Parallels

Joseph is one of the many biblical characters whose life was shattered by other people's sins. His half-brothers hated him so much that they threw him into a pit (Heb. *bor*; Gen 37:20). This downward movement also has a symbolic meaning – Joseph lost his high status. A rich man's favourite son became a slave, a nobody. He was stripped of his glory, just as he was stripped of his designer robe (Gen 37:3, 23). He was sold into slavery, and the merchants who bought him "go down to Egypt" (Gen 37:25), where Joseph's descent into the depth of suffering continued. Falsely accused, he lost the privileged position in his master's house and was sent to prison. Yet again, this descent was accompanied by losing his clothes, which were used for deceitful purposes against him (Gen 37:32–33; 39:12–16).

Later in the story, God used Pharaoh and his servants to bring Joseph out of jail: "Then Pharaoh sent and called Joseph, and they quickly brought him out of the pit" (Gen 41:14). In Hebrew, there are several words that could be used to describe a prison. But when reporting these events, the author, inspired by God, chose the strange word *bor*, which is literally "pit"[9] – and he seems to be playing with both literal and metaphorical meanings. Joseph's descent began when his brothers threw him into a dry well. Thirteen years later,[10] God lifted him up from the "pit". The upward movement is incredibly fast (no wonder it symbolizes resurrection): Joseph's transition from prison to palace happened in one day. And just as Joseph had lost two pieces of clothing on his way down, he gained at least two new sets of clothes on the way up. First, his prison clothes were exchanged for something more suitable to wear in Pharaoh's presence

---

8. According to Keener, "courageous, heroic, and honorable death was an ancient Mediterranean virtue, a virtue soon to be illustrated in John's Passion Narrative ... Because the Greek world highly regarded laying down one's life for another or for one's nation ... Greeks or Romans would readily grasp the early Christian concept that Jesus died 'on their behalf,' with or without the benefit of understanding atonement in the Levitical system." Keener, *Commentary*, 1005. There is, however, an important difference between Jesus and many war heroes who marched to their deaths: Jesus also showed perfect humility, and his heroism was completely free of hubris.

9. Even in prison, Joseph was placed in a position of authority (Gen 39:21–23), and he had access to Pharaoh's VIP prisoners. It is very unlikely that he was literally living in some kind of "pit" or dungeon.

10. Genesis 37:2; 41:46.

(Gen 41:14). Second, he was given attire that reflected his new status as second after Pharaoh (41:40).

Joseph's narrative can be summarized as a story of someone who went from a privileged position to a place of great power and glory – but his path led through the pit.

> I waited patiently for the LORD
> > he inclined to me and heard my cry.
> He drew me up from the pit [Heb. *bor*] of destruction,
> > out of the miry bog,
> and set my feet upon a rock,
> > making my steps secure.
> He put a new song in my mouth,
> > a song of praise to our God.
> Many will see and fear,
> > and put their trust in the LORD. (Ps 40:1–3)

The way up leads downwards. This great paradox of glory is reflected in the lives of many other OT saints and is particularly evident in the Gospel of John.

When East Becomes West

In the previous section, we saw that a V-shaped symbolical movement is discernible in the gospels and other NT books. This symbolism helps us to understand the paradox of Jesus's suffering: he descended in order to ascend. The same path is prepared for Jesus's disciples: we go down in order to be raised up; we die in order to be resurrected from the dead; we suffer shame in order to be glorified.

What about John and his gospel? Did John see the suffering of Christ in exactly the same way? It is my contention that he did not.

In the Gospel of John, Jesus's ascent to glory is viewed in a unique way. A reader of the Synoptic Gospels may say that Jesus was subject to humiliation and then glorified – first the cross, then the glory. But, in the Fourth Gospel, Jesus was glorified as he went to the cross. Crucifixion *is* the glorification of the Son of God.

Is there a contradiction between John and the Synoptics (and the rest of the NT authors)? No, there is not. Here, I will try to explain how both views of the passion of Christ can be true. Instead of contradicting each other, they supplement and enrich each other. These are rather abstract concepts, so an illustration using concrete historical characters may prove to be a helpful analogy.

In 1914, when World War I began, the Belgian army had some impressive weapons: armoured vehicles that were rare in the early stages of the Great War. Yet, this cutting-edge technology of the day turned out to be quite useless because the Western Front got stuck in trench warfare. Armoured trucks could do nothing in those trenches and in the mud between them. So, the vehicles and their crews went to fight on the Eastern Front. They travelled by sea to the Russian port of Archangelsk and joined the Russian army in fighting the Austro-Hungarian Empire (in modern West Ukraine). Since the Eastern Front was less static, the armoured vehicles made a significant contribution to the allied effort. In 1917, however, Russia collapsed and sank into a civil war. Germans and Austrians took control of vast territories that used to belong to the Russian Empire, and the Belgians found themselves trapped. They could not go home. The Central Powers now controlled the entire area from the North Sea to the Black Sea. Travelling west was impossible.

The Belgians made a decision that might, at first, seem absurd. They destroyed their vehicles – to prevent Bolsheviks getting hold of them – and went east. They travelled more than 10,000 kilometres, through a land where human laws no longer applied and God's commandments were forgotten. They kept going through the country that had been devastated by bands of marauders and murderers.

If we were to trace their journey on a regular map, we would notice that every day they travelled farther away from home. But they knew what they were doing. Finally, they reached Vladivostok, boarded a ship, crossed the Pacific Ocean, and landed in California. Then they journeyed through the United States – all the way to the East Coast – where they boarded another ship across the Atlantic Ocean to Britain and then to Belgium. Their journey home turned out to be a round-the-world adventure.

There are different kinds of maps of the world, but most of those maps clearly show Belgium in the west and Ukraine in the east. Still, it is possible to draw a map where Ukraine would be in the west and Belgium in the east. It would be a very strange map indeed, with North America and two oceans in the middle, yet such a strange map would not be false and would help us trace the Belgian legionnaires' painfully slow progress as they headed home.

In the Gospel of John, we have a somewhat peculiar map of glory and shame. In this map, we see Jesus returning home, to his Father's glory. Every step on the *Via Dolorosa* brought Jesus closer to that glory – the glory he had before the creation of the world (John 17:5). In the eyes of most people who witnessed his crucifixion, the cross was the very opposite of being glorified; for John, however, this is the way of glory.

John's "map" is just as accurate as those of the other evangelists, but it is not the same map. Although the Fourth Gospel gives us a view that is somewhat different from that of the Synoptics, it is a view of the same reality. John's gospel, if properly understood, gives us some awesome insights into God's glory. But how does one gain a pair of eyes capable of seeing that glory? After all, even many of the characters in the gospel failed to see it. What does it take to be able to see God's glory in the suffering of Christ and Christians? Perhaps putting ourselves in the situation of one of the characters in John's gospel will help us come closer to the answers to these questions.

Martha's Choice

Martha was a godly woman who had a strong faith. She confessed this faith even in the face of a terrible loss (John 11:27). This faith, however, was not perfect, and we see some of its limitations in the well-known story of Lazarus being raised from the dead. When Jesus was about to resurrect his friend, Martha objected:

> Jesus said, "Take away the stone." Martha, the sister of the dead man, said to him, "Lord, by this time there will be an odour, for he has been dead four days." Jesus said to her, "Did I not tell you that if you believed you would see the glory of God?" (John 11:39–40)

Martha's objection is easy to understand; humanly speaking, we can identify with her fear. Under "normal" circumstances, without the Son of God present, opening the grave would have resulted in additional shame and distress for Martha and most other people present. What is not so easy to understand is Jesus's answer to her objection.

Martha was about to witness a great miracle. Her faith – or lack of faith – would not affect the fact that Lazarus would be raised from the dead because Jesus had already decided to do so and announced his decision (see 11:11). Martha would see a great miracle whether or not she had faith. But would she see in this miracle God's glory? That is an open question. Much depended on her faith. According to John, it is quite possible to see a miracle without seeing God's glory.[11]

---

11. As Jesus himself said, for example, in John 6:36.

Whether or not Martha would see God's glory in her brother's resurrection depended largely on whether or not she believed in the words of Jesus that had no doubt been communicated to her: "But when Jesus heard it he said, 'This illness does not lead to death. It is for the glory of God, so that the Son of God may be glorified through it'" (11:4). So far, this promise had not been fulfilled since God's glory is the opposite of death and decay.[12] But now, Jesus was about to fulfil the promise and reveal God's glory. The only question was whether Martha would understand that his promise was being fulfilled.

Here we come to the essence of the faith of the NT saints. When people look at the mighty deeds done by Christ, they may see miracles. But only those who have faith can see the fulfilment of God's promise. This kind of faith affirms that God spoke in the past, that he gave very specific promises, that he is worthy of trust, and that his promises are fulfilled in Jesus. When such faith is absent, it is tantamount to affirming that God did not really speak through the OT prophets, that he spoke but without giving any specific promises, that he promised but is not strong enough or caring enough to fulfil those promises, or that his promises will be fulfilled someday but not in Jesus from Nazareth.

It is the presence or absence of this kind of faith that makes the difference between seeing God's glory and remaining blind to it – and, eventually, persisting in this blindness like the Pharisees (John 9:40–41). If we have this kind of faith, it can be strengthened and cultivated by reading the gospels in the light of the OT promises.

Did Martha see God's glory in Lazarus's resurrection? John does not answer this question, and one can only hope that she did. We do not know much about Martha's life, but it is safe to assume that her brother's death was one of the lowest points in that life. And then, things got worse when Jesus made her suffer shame in front of many people (John 11:19): she was just standing and not doing anything as the stone was being rolled away from her brother's grave. Her inaction was probably considered highly shameful – until the moment Lazarus walked out of the grave.

Then, of course, when Lazarus was raised from the dead, this brought Martha much joy. One can see a V-shaped symbolic movement in her life: first she goes down into gloom and despair, then she is lifted up into God's glory. The road up first goes down.

Martha could not see God's glory on her way down. But if she saw the connection between God's promise and its fulfilment, she would see this

---

12. In the laws of cleanliness and holiness given in the book of Leviticus, death is seen as the worst kind of defilement. These laws emphasize that death is the opposite of God's holiness.

glory on her way up. What about us, modern readers? Do we see Lazarus's resurrection as just a miracle? Or do we see it, as John intended, as a display of God's glory – the fulfilment of Jesus's promise? In the next chapter, we will discuss some ways in which John helps us see God's glory.

Summary

The Gospel of John has much to say about the future of the children of God. This future is full of God's glory and, in John's realized eschatology, much of that glory can be seen even now.

Jesus's disciples were torn individuals, many of whom were traumatized by the rejection from their relatives and religious leaders. Yet, they were able to see God's glory – not just *in spite* of these difficult circumstances but *in* them and *through* them. This paradoxical truth is illustrated by the example of the former blind man who was rejected by the synagogue rulers. They tried to intimidate him into slandering Jesus, but he courageously testified to the truth – and that was how he gave glory to God. When he was driven out of the synagogue, Jesus found him and led him into a deeper truth about the Son of God.

Those who follow Jesus, whether in the first or twenty-first centuries, are given a new pair of eyes, so to speak – an ability to give a new and meaningful interpretation to reality, particularly a radically new interpretation of Jesus's death. Many people view Jesus's crucifixion as a tragedy and, since we often feel like victims, it can be comforting to see him as a victim too. But Jesus himself rejected this interpretation of his death, and John helps his readers "see" that Jesus's death was not a tragedy. Jesus is not a victim but a conqueror: he overcame by dying for God's glory. The Synoptic Gospels portray Jesus as being glorified after his descent into the valley of humiliation. The Gospel of John depicts Jesus as being glorified *during* his crucifixion. There is, however, no ultimate contradiction between the gospels: those two views of God's glory are not mutually exclusive if one appreciates the paradoxical nature of John's eschatological approach.

Those who are able to interpret Jesus's death in this way can also see God's glory in many other contexts. The example of Martha, however, shows that this new vision – this ability to interpret reality in terms of God's glory – does not come automatically. While born-again children of God are given this ability, they often must choose whether or not to use it. Much depends on whether they understand the history of salvation – and their own part in it – as fulfilment of God's promises. Understanding this enables them to rejoice even in the most difficult circumstances.

4

The Eyes That See God's Glory

Jesus gives his followers eyes that see God's glory – something that the world is so often blind to. Before moving on to examine the things that this new vision allows us to perceive, let us consider what seems to be the most difficult situation in which to see God's glory. John needed to persuade his readers that crucifixion – the most shameful treatment possible in the ancient world – did in fact manifest God's glory. How does John do this?

"Lifted Up" – in Shame or Glory?

One of John's favourite ways to express irony has to do with polysemy – playing with different meanings of a word. Before analyzing specific examples from his gospel, I will try to show how polysemy works in the OT. Let us consider another example from Joseph's story.

When Joseph was in jail, he interpreted the dreams of two of Pharaoh's officials. While these dreams predicted two very different outcomes, there are also similarities between them. When Joseph explained the meanings of those dreams, he used the Hebrew word *yissa*, which is a form of the verb that means "to lift up." Joseph promised the chief butler that Pharaoh would lift up his head, using this expression in a metaphorical way: "In three days Pharaoh will lift up your head and restore you to your office, and you shall place Pharaoh's cup in his hand as formerly, when you were his cupbearer" (Gen 40:13).

Joseph then made another prediction of a totally different kind. The expression "lift up your head" is used with a literal meaning in Joseph's promise to the chief baker: "In three days Pharaoh will lift up your head – from you! – and hang you on a tree" (Gen 40:19). The content of these two predictions could not be more different. Yet, the form has remarkable similarities. Surely

Joseph[1] could have used other words to make his point, but he did not. The two radically different outcomes explained in this dream have more in common than what initially seems to be the case. This remarkable unity of form comes from the fact that both outcomes are in the hand of the one God who has sovereign power over everything that happens in this world.

Three days later, Joseph's predictions came true: "On the third day, which was Pharaoh's birthday, he made a feast for all his servants and lifted up the head of the chief cupbearer and the head of the chief baker among his servants" (Gen 40:20). Two heads were lifted up – but the lifting up of one's head can mean either honourable restoration (glorification) or dishonourable death.

This example helps to illustrate a truth that is very important for John: things are not as they appear. Not always.

A similar ambiguity (although much more subtle) can be found in the prophecy of Isaiah: "Behold, my servant shall act wisely; he shall be high and lifted up [*nissa*], and shall be exalted" (Isa 52:13). What is the meaning of the word translated as "lifted up" in this passage? Clearly, the verse predicts glorification of the servant of Yahweh. But does it offer any hints about the way in which he will be glorified? Can the verb *nissa* have a literal meaning as well? According to John, both literal and metaphorical meanings are implied here, which would explain the very abrupt transition to the next verse in Isaiah: "As many were astonished at you – his appearance was so marred, beyond human semblance, and his form beyond that of the children of mankind" (52:14). The prophet speaks about the Messiah's suffering, disfigurement, and dishonour; and then, in the following verse, he makes another transition, another contrast that is just as stark, as he returns to the theme of glory, revelation, and universal conquest: "so shall he [startle] many nations; kings shall shut their mouths because of him; for that which has not been told them they see, and that which they have not heard they understand" (52:15).

Glory, revelation, and conquering the world are themes that are intertwined and developed in the Gospel of John, and the verb "lift up" (ὑψόω, *hupsoo*) – the Greek equivalent of the Hebrew *yissa* – is the key that unlocks an important dimension in John's theology of glory.

Jesus said, "'And I, when I am lifted up [ὑψωθῶ, *hupsotho*] from the earth, will draw all people to myself.' He said this to show by what kind of death he was going to die" (John 12:32–33). Here, John shares with the readers his post-resurrection perspective. He explains to us something that he understood only

---

1. And the author who, inspired by God, reproduced the content of that conversation in Hebrew.

after Jesus was raised from the dead. He puts us, his readers, in the privileged position of being able to understand what John himself did not understand when he heard Jesus speak those words.

The crowds who listened to Jesus in chapter 12 had no idea what the verb "lifted up" meant in that particular context. They seemed to grasp some of the metaphorical meaning of the word ὑψωθῶ (*hupsotho*) – which implies honour and glory. But they did not know that Jesus was referring to his crucifixion – to being literally, physically lifted up. Just like Pharaoh's servants, who did not understand the meaning of their own dreams until Joseph explained it to them, Jesus's audience could not understand the meaning of the word they heard until Jesus was raised from the dead – in the light of that resurrection, everything changes.

This is how John manages to combine two meanings that seem incompatible. He shows that on the cross of Jesus, God's glory was revealed in a visible, tangible way and made public and universal. Yet, this was not obvious, which is why those who did not seek God did not see this glory.

Post-Resurrection Perspective

Jesus helped his suffering disciples in more ways than can be counted. One of the most important ways in which he did so was by strengthening their hope – by teaching them to see their circumstances from a post-resurrection perspective. Since the power of hope is not obvious, in this section, I will discuss what hope is and what it does. Perhaps it is better to start with the latter aspect. Using examples from modern life, I will show how hope can make the difference between life and death, between defeat and victory. Then we will see how the biblical concept of hope goes beyond what is usually meant by the word "hope" in the English language in the twenty-first century.

Secular and Biblical Concepts of Hope

The fallen world is full of suffering, a biblical truth that is amply supported by many examples from the twentieth century. During World War II, Viktor Frankl, an Austrian psychologist, survived the horrors of a Nazi concentration camp in Auschwitz. In describing his experience in a book, he discusses the difference between those who survived and those who gave up. He notes that, often, that difference had little to do with physical strength and health. Strong people would break down and give up, while some not-so-strong ones endured everything. According to Frankl, it was hope and meaning that made the greatest difference: those who had something to live for also had hope, and that hope carried them through the darkest hours of Auschwitz. Frankl gives a fascinating account of how this was true in his own life.

> I remember a personal experience. Almost in tears from pain . . . I limped a few kilometers with our long column of men from the camp to our work site. Very cold, bitter winds struck us. I kept thinking of the endless little problems of our miserable life. What would there be to eat tonight? If a piece of sausage came as extra ration, should I exchange it for a piece of bread? . . . How could I get a piece of wire to replace the fragment which served as one of my shoelaces? . . .
>
> I became disgusted with the state of affairs which compelled me, daily and hourly, to think of only such trivial things. I forced my thoughts to turn to another subject. Suddenly I saw myself standing on the platform of a well-lit, warm and pleasant lecture room. In front of me sat an attentive audience on comfortable upholstered seats. I was giving a lecture on the psychology of the concentration camp! All that oppressed me at that moment became objective, seen and described from the remote viewpoint of science. By this method I succeeded somehow in rising above the situation, above the sufferings of the moment, and I observed them as if they were already of the past. Both I and my troubles became the object of an interesting psychoscientific study undertaken by myself.[2]

Hope makes us stronger. But how exactly does it do that? Frankl's experience shows that hope makes us stronger by changing the way we view things. When the observation point changes, something changes within the observer as well. Someone who can change their point of view in this way – even if just for a few seconds – exercises some power over their own thinking. At that moment, they cease to be victims.

Frankl's discovery helps us to understand the nature of hope. Hope is expectation of a good outcome in the future. Hope is always related to the future, but a hopeful view of the future makes a difference in the present. When the NT authors speak about the suffering of Christians, they often emphasize the temporal nature of that suffering (Rom 8:18).

---

2. Frankl, *Man's Search*, 94.

Frankl himself, although he had a deep understanding of some biblical themes and concepts, was not a practising Christian. While there is no reason Christians should not learn from his experience, it is important to note that Christian hope goes further – much further. Frankl's hope was based on two elements: imagination and desire. This is how "hope" is usually understood in the modern English-speaking world – something good but, unfortunately, without any guarantee that it will ever happen. When the NT writers speak about hope, however, they mean something much better. Our hope for eternal life is based on God's promise, which cannot be broken. This hope can lift us above our circumstances, no matter how ugly they are.

A prisoner can ask himself, "What will this situation look like when I, liberated from the concentration camp, give a lecture in a university?" Even a short reflection on this question can make a great difference because this alternative observation point is very high indeed. A Christian has access to some even higher vantage points. Ignatius of Loyola, the founder of the Jesuit order, taught his followers to review, every evening, all the events of the day and then ask themselves what these events might look like in the last minutes of their life.

This change of perspective fits with the reminders in the Gospel of John that time is short – both for service and for suffering.[3] But the change of perspective in John takes place on a much grander scale. The Fourth Evangelist leads the readers to see their lives from a post-resurrection point of view. When going through a trial, we can ask, "What will this look like when we are raised from the dead?" To understand this principle, let us start with the resurrection of Jesus.

Jesus's Resurrection Changes the Disciples' Perspective

Jesus said and did many things that his contemporaries found hard to understand. For example, when he cleansed the temple, even his disciples did not understand the meaning of that action. The words he spoke seemed to increase their confusion rather than clarify anything: "Destroy this temple, and in three days I will raise it up" (John 2:19). But when he rose from the dead, it became clear to them that he had spoken about the temple of his body (2:21–22).

When Jesus spoke about the Holy Spirit to the crowds at the feast, nobody could understand what he meant (7:39). But after his resurrection, after the

---

3. See, for example, John 9:4; 11:9–10.

disciples received the Holy Spirit, they were finally able to grasp the meaning of the words he had spoken earlier. Now they could access and interpret their memories from a privileged position, from a post-resurrection vantage point.

Being able to read the Gospel of John is a great privilege. The author allows the readers to enter his own privileged position. He gives us an opportunity to view the events described in the text from a post-resurrection perspective. For example, when we read in John 2:19 about the disciples struggling to understand, we are given the privileged information of John 2:21–22 so that, in some way, we can understand their experience better than they themselves could at the time.

The experience of meeting the risen Christ greatly changed the disciples' way of thinking. Things that might have seemed meaningless just a few hours before – for example, the crucifixion – now become integral parts of God's plan to save the world.[4] It is this experience that made them reject the "tragic" interpretation of Jesus's death (see chapter 3, section titled "Jesus's Death: Not a Tragedy").

In a similar – though not the same – way, the disciples learned to view their own experience of suffering and rejection as bringing glory to God rather than as something meaningless and "tragic." Before the passion of Christ, we see how they struggled with much of Jesus's teaching because they failed to understand his imminent resurrection.

One of the most ironic examples of such misunderstanding can be found in John 11. Jesus wanted the disciples to go with him to Judea to witness the resurrection of Lazarus and, later, his own resurrection. He knew that when they saw God's glory revealed in these mighty deeds, they would be filled with joy. But since the disciples did not yet have an adequate faith, they received Jesus's invitation to go back to Judea with great reluctance. The "gloom and doom" interpretation they gave to his words made them respond in an ironically twisted way. Although Jesus was "glad" for their sake (11:15), they did not share any of that gladness, and they went to Judea with the resignation

---

4. When I use the expression "saving the world," I do not give it a universalist meaning ("everyone will be saved"). The well-known verse that speaks about God's love for "the world" (John 3:16) mentions salvation for those who believe, not for everyone. But when God saves believing individuals, he also provides for them a suitable environment: a world full of his gifts that satisfy human needs. He does not save bodiless souls who have no cultural memories. He saves human beings whose existence has both physical and spiritual dimensions. As for the wicked in this present torn world, their fate seems to be so irrelevant to many aspects of life in the new Jerusalem that it is possible to speak of them as not belonging to – or, to use a Semitic idiom, "having no part in" – the renewed world, which is cleansed from sin and all its consequences.

of prisoners sentenced to a meaningless death: "So Thomas, called the Twin, said to his fellow disciples, 'Let us also go, that we may die with him'" (11:16).

The disciples' attitude, however, changed radically after they met the resurrected Christ and received the Holy Spirit. In a similar way, many followers of Christ in the twenty-first century often struggle and fail because of our weak faith in resurrection, including our own resurrection. It is not that the disciples did not have any faith – they certainly did (2:11b). Yet, that faith was still lacking in many ways. John himself explains that, until that Easter Sunday evening, their faith did not have a firm scriptural foundation: "for as yet they did not understand the Scripture, that he must rise from the dead" (20:9).

The disciples' pre-Easter faith seemed to be based on the miraculous signs they saw.[5] There is nothing wrong with this, but Jesus was not content to leave them with this kind of faith. He patiently led them towards a Scripture-based faith. Now John the Evangelist seems to be doing the same for some of his readers: those who already believe in Christ who "was raised on the third day" may still need to be rooted in faith in Christ who "was raised on the third day *in accordance with the Scriptures*" (1 Cor 15:4; emphasis added).

This observation is relevant to a question that needs to be asked here: How can we make this transition towards a Scripture-based faith? For example, we read in Acts that when Peter and John were beaten by the Jewish authorities, they rejoiced instead of being dejected (5:40–41). Such joy is, of course, an expression of a robust, mature faith. These disciples came to such a strong faith after Jesus himself appeared to them. But what about us? How can we progress towards such strength and maturity without having seen the resurrected Christ? Jesus said, "Blessed are those who have not seen and yet have believed" (John 20:29). Our main question is, "How do we attain such a blessed state?"

The answer that I venture to offer is both simple and complex. It is simple because it can be summed up in one sentence: The Gospel of John encourages us to reject a "tragic" interpretation of our own torn experience and teaches us to see our own life as a quest for God's glory. It is complex because implementing this change requires a great deal of wisdom.

It is here that many simplistic approaches to the Bible and to life fail. Some Christians assert that all the answers to life's greatest questions are found in the Bible. While this is certainly true, finding those answers is not necessarily easy because we have to look for them in a massive and complex collection of ancient texts produced in a totally different cultural setting. And even when we

---

5. Note the close connection between signs and faith in John 2:11: "This, the first of his signs, Jesus did at Cana in Galilee, and manifested his glory. And his disciples believed in him."

find the right answer, we still have to apply it to our own life in a torn world, where our circumstances are often very complicated. For example, Proverbs 26:4–5 instructs us: "Answer not a fool according to his folly, lest you be like him yourself. Answer a fool according to his folly, lest he be wise in his own eyes." There are apparently two different methods of dealing with fools, but it takes wisdom to know which situations in our life require the former approach ("answer not") and which situations call for the latter method ("answer").

Applying Scripture to our own lives can be compared to the art of playing a musical instrument. The biblical text is like the sheet music, and our daily choices are like the musical keys. The music score explains precisely which key needs to be pressed and for how long, but the piece we are trying to play may turn out to be extremely difficult – something that requires years of practice. Well-meaning but naïve Christians who insist that "all the answers are in the Bible" can be compared to adults who make a first-grader sit at the piano with a very difficult piece and expect the child to play it well because, after all, "it is all written there" and one just has to play the notes and not deviate from them.

Many of our failures in daily life come not from a lack of faith in the sufficiency of the Scripture but, rather, from a lack of the wisdom and experience required to apply the Scripture. Jesus promised those Jews who believed in him, "If you abide in my word, you are truly my disciples, and you will know the truth, and the truth will set you free" (John 8:31–32). This promised liberation is not likely to be quick and easy. It takes a great deal of time and practice to "abide" in his word, even for those who are committed to make this word the centre of their lives.

Earlier I discussed the example of a psychologist who was able to catch a glimpse of freedom in a concentration camp. At best, human effort can produce only glimpses of such freedom. To be able to consistently view one's torn life in a different way, the way of God's glory, disciples must undergo a major change in worldview. They have to make some progress from faith based on experience – such as seeing "signs" – to faith based on Scripture. In the next section, we will look at how Jesus gave his disciples a new understanding of the OT as a whole.

Our lives can also be compared to texts that we keep interpreting, and we can learn to reject the "tragic" interpretations in favour of those that make God's glory central; but to do this, we must learn to interpret the Bible. It is only after the disciples had mastered a Christ-centred interpretation of the OT that they became skilful interpreters of the "text" of their own lives. To those who believe, Jesus gives an ability to see in the spiritual darkness of this world (8:12). However, these "night-vision devices" require practice if they are to work properly and must be properly "tuned" by studying the Scripture. In fact, without Scripture, they hardly work at all.

As Martha stood at her brother's seemingly violated grave, she was confronted with a challenge: how could she see God's glory in these shameful circumstances? The answer is implied in Jesus's rhetorical question: "Did I not tell you that if you believed you would see the glory of God?" (John 11:40).

Sometime before, Martha had received a promise: "This illness does not lead to death. It is for the glory of God, so that the Son of God may be glorified through it" (11:4).[6] Would she view what Jesus did as fulfilment of his earlier promise? Like many grieving people, Martha was probably overwhelmed with conflicting thoughts and feelings, but she still had to choose between two interpretations of what was happening: a tragedy or a revelation of God's glory. She could have viewed it as a "tragedy" (in the sense discussed in the section "Post-Resurrection Perspective"). Such an interpretation would portray Jesus as a tragic figure who could not prevent Lazarus's tragedy and then, for some strange reason, made another tragic mistake by opening a grave – something that would have been viewed as a shameful action that brought much dishonour both to the person who did this and to the family of the deceased.

After Lazarus was raised from the dead, Martha still had to choose between two interpretations: either what happened was just a miracle or it was a sign giving glory to God. While the former interpretation would not be entirely wrong, it is the latter that reflects a mature faith. When we read the Scriptures, there is a great difference between seeing Jesus as simply doing wondrous deeds and seeing Jesus as fulfilling God's promises.

Now let us consider how Jesus himself interpreted those promises given in the OT.

The New Understanding of Scripture

In the Gospel of John, we have Jesus quoting the OT seven times. Although this is a relatively small number, this does not mean that the OT was not important

---

6. In my opinion, these words are best understood as addressed not only to the disciples but also to the messenger(s) who brought the news about Lazarus's sickness to Jesus (11:3).

for John. Quite the opposite. When one considers the number of OT allusions[7] and echoes[8] present in the Fourth Gospel, it is hard to disagree with Hanson:

> For the author of the Fourth Gospel scripture is not just a prop, an addition. It is constitutive for this work. Indeed we may guess that one of the main reasons that he wrote his gospel was that he wanted to show to what extent the career and person of Jesus Christ was the fulfilment of scripture . . . Far more than any of the other three, this Gospel is concerned with scripture and the fulfilment of scripture . . . The author of the Fourth Gospel . . . excelled at his understanding to what extent the prophecies of scripture have been fulfilled in Jesus. Perhaps this is something of what Clement of Alexandria meant when he called it "the spiritual Gospel."[9]

Analyzing every instance where Jesus or John quote the OT would be far beyond the scope of this book, but here I would like to focus on two questions that are directly related to our study: How did Jesus interpret the OT as a whole? How did this interpretation that he passed on to his disciples differ from, for example, the interpretations that had been developed by the rabbis in John's time?

A simple answer to these questions is that for the rabbis who lived after AD 70, the OT – especially the law of Moses – was increasingly becoming a book of rules. For Jesus and his disciples, it was a book of promises. That was probably the main difference. Of course, many non-messianic Jews in John's day were also trying to focus on God's promises in the Hebrew Bible, but it was hard for them to see how those promises were going to be fulfilled in a situation where the temple had been destroyed and the Jews had lost the opportunity to

---

7. There is no scholarly consensus on what exactly constitutes an allusion, but here I use the criteria offered by Beal: there has to be "incomparable or unique parallel in wording, syntax, concept, or cluster of motifs in the same order or structure." Beale, *Handbook*, 31.

8. Not all commentators distinguish between allusions and echoes, but Daly-Denton's explanation of the difference seems quite helpful: "While quotations are clearly made intentionally, echoes are spontaneous evocations of existing texts. While an allusion usually has fairly substantial volume (a phrase or at least several words in common with the precursor text), an echo may be quite fleeting, often not more than one word . . . Attentiveness to echo can enable us to hear some of the resonances with which a work such as the fourth gospel resounded for its original audience. We will find that an ear attuned to echoes can discern layers of intratextual reference that greatly enhance our appreciation of John's Gospel." Daly-Denton, "Psalms in John's Gospel," 120.

9. Hanson, *Prophetic Gospel*, 253.

live in much of the promised land. Moreover, for John, the OT was not just a book of promises but a book of promises fulfilled in Jesus Christ.[10]

In the secularized mainstream cultures of much of the modern world, too, the Bible is often viewed as a book of rules – usually prohibitions. Even Christians may sometimes unwittingly contribute to this truncated view of the Bible when they read it with a heavy emphasis on guidance for their daily lives and ministries, seeking answers to the question "What shall we do for God?" While this is, of course, an essential element in any responsible Bible study, it should not eclipse another indispensable dimension of Scripture as a book about what God has done for his glory. One of the main ways in which God is glorified is through fulfilling his promises.

The entire OT, from beginning to end, is a book that witnesses to God's faithfulness. When we study Jesus's attitude to Scripture in the Gospel of John, it is helpful to remember that he often referred to large sections of the OT and, sometimes, to the OT in its entirety. For example, when alluding to the resurrection of dry bones,[11] Jesus did not refer just to a few verses in Ezekiel 37 but to the entire corpus of Ezekiel's prophecies about the restoration of Israel. When he spoke about rivers of living water (John 7:37–38), his promises are based on large sections of Isaiah, Ezekiel, Zechariah, and Joel. He treated the prophets' writings as a whole unit. When Jesus explained that Moses wrote about him (5:45–46), his explanation has to do not just with some isolated verses from the Torah but with the entire collection of the written law.[12] Although commentators like to discuss which biblical author Jesus (and John) quoted most often,[13] throughout the Fourth Gospel, Jesus referred to the Scripture as a whole. According to Schuchard,

> John's Old Testament citations are admittedly few in number. John obviously makes no attempt with his citations to exhaust the connections that could have been made between the person and

---

10. Of course, John understood that some of those promises were still awaiting fulfilment (see John 21:22a, where Jesus mentioned his second coming), but the general emphasis of his theology is on the promise fulfilled (or being fulfilled).

11. Such allusions can be detected both in John 3:5–8 and John 5:25. See also Köstenberger, *John*, 219.

12. Like many of his contemporaries, John also sometimes used the word "law" to mean the whole OT – not only the *Torah* but also *Neviim* (meaning "Prophets") and *Ketuvim* (meaning "Writings"). For example, in John 10:34 Jesus quotes from the Psalms and refers to it as "[the] Law."

13. According to Moyise, about half the quotations come from Psalms; four quotations are from Isaiah, two from Zechariah, and one (or possibly two) from Exodus. Moyise, *Old Testament*, 92.

work of Jesus and the Old Testament. Still . . . whenever John refers to a particular passage from the Old Testament, it is always *the entire* Old Testament, the body of God's revelation given through Moses and passed on from generation to generation, which is also in view. Thus, John employs Old Testament citations as discreet, concrete illustrations of his Gospel's larger scheme to convey John's conviction that the entire Old Testament testifies to Jesus (5:39, 45–46). Jesus, therefore, has fulfilled all of Scripture and is himself its ultimate significance.[14]

When Jesus opens the eyes of his followers – whether literally or metaphorically – one of the most important things they begin to see is the OT Scripture in its messianic interpretation. Reading the OT without faith at the end of the first century AD would have been a very confusing experience, accompanied by questions that were hard to answer:

- What happened to God's great promises about restoring Israel? Have they been left unfulfilled?
- What about Haggai's promise that the glory of the Second Temple (now destroyed) would be greater than the glory of Solomon's Temple (Haggai 2:9)?
- Did God change his mind, so to speak?
- Why did he bring the Jews back from Babylon six centuries before only to disperse them again?

Without the promised Messiah, the history of OT Israel does not seem to make much sense.

As Jesus separated his faithful followers from "the world," he separated them from this perception of their own nation's history as "unfulfilled" and gave them a new understanding of what Scripture does: it witnesses. It bears witness to Jesus (John 5:39).

To describe the experience of the disciples who began to see the OT as a witness to Christ, one can use Menken's terminology – his use of the contrasts "before" and "after," form and content: "before the coming of Jesus, Scripture remains, so to speak, 'empty'; Jesus is the reality that fills the words of Scripture. Before his coming, the words of Scripture constitute a promise of a reality that is not yet present on earth; they refer to someone who is not yet there."[15]

---

14. Schuchard, *Scripture within Scripture*, 155–56; emphasis added.
15. Menken, "Significance," 162.

This understanding of Jesus's ministry as fulfilment of the entire OT is another way in which Jesus separated his followers from "the world." Their persecutors were religious people who professed to have a high respect for God's law. But their interpretation of that law was so different that Jesus used second- and third-person pronouns when he spoke about their attitude to the OT: "your Law" (10:34) and "their Law" (15:25). He did not refer to it as "our Law" or teach his disciples to do so. Instead, he taught them to speak about their persecutors as a separate group, with its own values and its own, very different, interpretation of Scripture.

Without Jesus, the history of OT Israel is truly tragic. With Jesus as the Messiah, this history, painful as it is, ceases to be just a tragedy and becomes a story of God's glory. As the disciples learned to read Scripture in this way, this prepared them for a new interpretation of their own lives. Before moving on to this new interpretation – which is the subject of chapters 5 and 6 – I will discuss some parallels between first-century and twenty-first-century disciples and consider some unique features of the situation faced by all followers of Jesus.

The Disciples as a Group

The Gospel of John seems to be one of those books that travel easily across cultural boundaries. People from various ethnic and social groups have been drawn to John's testimony, finding in it hope and meaning for their own lives. Because of John's relatively simple style, his narrative is much easier to read than, for example, the Epistle to the Hebrews. But that simplicity can be misleading. As one delves deeper into the Fourth Gospel, it proves to be an extremely complex text, full of exegetical challenges. John's main message is simple – even a child can understand it. But some aspects of John's teaching are enormously difficult even for those Bible interpreters who have dedicated their whole lives to studying this gospel.

In the second half of the twentieth century, as scholars began paying more attention to the Jewish background of John, new questions began to surface. One of these questions has to do with the extent of biblical literacy that John seemed to have expected his original audience to have.

Some interpreters assume that John wrote for Gentiles or proselytes, who had very little knowledge of Judaism. Otherwise, why would he feel the need to explain the meaning of such terms as "rabbi" (1:38) or "Messiah" (4:25)? That assumption is problematic because, as other interpreters point out, John often uses scriptural allusions that are very hard to detect even for readers with an extensive knowledge of the OT. But if readers were competent enough to understand the references to Ezekiel's vision and Daniel's revelation (combined in the reference to "son of man" in 1:51), why would they need an explanation of such basic Jewish terms?

The solution to this problem seems to involve rejecting the idea of some monolithic, heterogenous audience. Instead, John probably had in mind several different audiences with different experiences and needs. In the long run, he meant his gospel to have a global impact,[16] but he had a special interest in a group of torn readers who had been excommunicated from the synagogue.

If John wrote for several groups of readers, how were these groups related to one another? Several answers have been offered to this question, but Koester's suggestion seems to be the most helpful: when it comes to biblical literacy, different (potential) readers of the Fourth Gospel form a spectrum – from the least-informed to the most-informed.[17] Readers who believe the gospel and make meditation on the text an integral part of their lifestyle (John 8:31) will progress along the spectrum towards becoming better informed. For example, the "good shepherd" discourse (10:1–17) uses metaphors that virtually anyone living in the ancient Mediterranean culture could understand: a good shepherd is someone who protects and cares for the sheep (people) he loves. As readers become better acquainted with OT imagery and theology, they may realize that the shepherd often symbolizes God in his relationship with Israel. Those who are familiar with the prophetic literature and the history of Israel are also more likely to appreciate the contrast between the shepherds who feed only themselves (Ezek 34:2–6) and the promised Messiah.[18] The list of such examples could go on and on.

This progress along a continuum corresponds to being rooted in the truth of the gospel. This truth is multidimensional; and so, when we grow, we begin to understand new dimensions without negating our previous knowledge of the truth. This principle can be seen in the transformation experienced by the Samaritan woman in John 4. When the conversation began, she stated a fact: she was speaking with a Jewish man (4:9). As she got to know Jesus better, she identified him as a prophet (4:19). This was also a true statement, even though Jesus is much more than a prophet. As she discovered this new dimension of truth about Jesus, she did not need to reject her previous understanding of him as a Jewish man – that was still correct. When she acknowledged Jesus as

---

16. The Samaritans – who were not particularly interested in God's dealings with the Jewish people – proclaimed Jesus as "the Saviour of the world," not just of Israel (John 4:42).

17. Koester, "Spectrum," 9–11.

18. Koester, 12–18.

a prophet, he did what prophets often do and revealed to her his supernatural knowledge. That revelation enabled her to ascend to a greater truth: Jesus is the promised Messiah (4:25–26). But that new and greater truth – or rather, a new dimension of the same truth – did not make her previous true statements lose their value. Those statements, while incomplete, are not false.

When the Samaritan woman realized that Jesus was the Messiah, this realization transformed her both spiritually and socially.[19] She became a sort of missionary to the people of her town, but that did not mean that her understanding of Jesus's messiahship would never need to change. The Samaritan woman disappears from John's narrative; but we know from the experience of Jesus's other disciples that even after they confessed him to be the Christ or the Messiah, they still had to accept the fact that his messianic reign came with the cross (Matt 16:21–23), and that acceptance was painfully difficult for them. As the disciples learned new dimensions of truth about Jesus, they did not have to jettison previous truths about him. Yet, they did have to reject their false expectations about his messiahship and their own role in his kingdom.

The Gospel of John meets us where we are. It is accessible to people in all kinds of circumstances. John can speak powerfully even to readers who do not know much about the OT. But he does not want such readers to remain biblically illiterate. If they keep reading, they will move along Koester's continuum and keep gaining much deeper knowledge of the whole Bible.

As we read the gospel in a thoughtful and sincere way, it changes us. It gives us new insights into who we are, where we come from, and where we are going. It helps us understand the rest of Scripture. If and when we abide in the word of Jesus, we become more competent interpreters of the Bible and of our own lives. In this process, we will have to let go of some things in our life, including our unrealistic expectations.

The gospel changes, among other things, our relationship with the torn world. That change will not necessarily be painless – some readers are likely to become torn individuals as their witness will result in a diminished social status, with the accompanying burden of shame and ostracism. But the gospel also provides ways of dealing with that shame. Shame is countered with the glory of being children of God, and the pain of being excluded from the

---

19. Note the parallels between this Samaritan woman and Mary Magdalene (John 20:11–18). Both came to the place where they did not expect to meet Jesus. Both were lonely and broken when they arrived but left as "missionaries" who, at that point, understood Jesus's identity better than the rest of the disciples, at least to some extent.

synagogue – or some other important social structure – is alleviated by the joy of belonging to the community of resurrection, new birth, forgiveness, love, and hope.

"Already, but Not Yet"

The community of God's children is not physically isolated from the world. Disciples of Jesus may live in close proximity to their persecutors and share much of their social and cultural space with those who do not believe in Jesus. Yet, this community also finds itself in a unique situation where the future invades the present. The example of the ten disciples (that is, the twelve without Judas and also without Thomas – who joined them later) is a good illustration of this paradox.

Jesus was raised from the dead very early in the morning. Soon after, while it was still early morning, he appeared to Mary Magdalene and gave her a message for the disciples. She gladly obeyed; and early on that first Easter morning, the disciples heard that the Lord was risen from the dead (20:18).

Later on that day – much later, when it was already evening (20:19) – Jesus appeared to the disciples, and they finally saw him with their own eyes. Why did he choose to come to them in the evening? Obviously, he wanted them to spend several hours in that transitional state when they had *already* heard the good news of his resurrection but had *not yet* seen him. What was accomplished during this time? And what can we learn from this?

This passage seems relevant for modern readers because most of us are in a similar liminal[20] state. We have already heard the good news of Jesus's resurrection.[21] We have not yet seen him but we certainly will – most probably after our physical death, which may come sooner than we think. For some people, meeting Jesus face to face will be the most joyful event of their lives; for others, it will be their worst nightmare. This difference – and our eternal destiny – has to do with how we have responded to the testimony about Jesus's resurrection.

---

20. The term is derived from the Latin word *limen* (meaning, "threshold"). See Kok, "New Perspectives," 309–10; Brant, *John*, 171.

21. This is why, in my opinion, it is important to include reading Bible passages in the church service. When we hear the words of the apostles and prophets, a liminal situation is created, in which we are confronted with God's spoken words in "real-time mode."

Before we analyze our own response, let us see how the apostles[22] reacted to the good news of Jesus's resurrection that was preached to them. According to Luke, when Mary Magdalene and the other women shared the good news, the apostles "did not believe them."[23] They did learn an important lesson, though. Eventually, they would have to go through all the world, preaching the gospel to all nations – and the bodily resurrection of Jesus would be a key element of that gospel they preached. The idea of physical resurrection, however, was completely alien to the peoples of the Hellenistic world.[24] When the apostle Paul preached resurrection to the Greeks, they scoffed at him (Acts 17:18). Those long hours behind locked doors probably taught the disciples not to be easily discouraged when they had to deal with somebody's failure to believe in the resurrection. After all, having been in such a situation themselves, they should have remembered how unrealistic Magdalene's testimony had sounded to them.

That lesson was important, and the ten disciples had a whole week to learn it. Thomas, who was not with them when Jesus appeared in the room, refused to believe their testimony. No doubt the disciples repeated their story many times, giving Thomas the opportunity to learn about all the details of Jesus's appearance to them, but his disbelief was not caused by a lack of information provided by reliable witnesses. Thomas chose not to believe – or, to be precise, he chose to believe only on his own terms (20:25).

Thomas's disbelief ended when Jesus appeared to him. Until then, no amount of preaching or reasoning could make him change his mind. The story of Thomas's conversion reminds us that we cannot generate faith in the people to whom we preach. Conversion and regeneration are the work of the Holy Spirit. John's gospel lays much emphasis on witnessing and encourages its Christian readers to keep witnessing even in the most hostile environment, but it also frees them from taking responsibility for the outcome of that witness. The reaction of listeners – whether they accept or reject the apostolic testimony – is beyond the control of the disciples who bear witness. Their faithfulness to God and his mission is not measured by the number of converts.

---

22. John never uses this word for the disciples, although he does speak of "the twelve" (6:70–71). But here, we are also looking at passages from the other gospels.

23. "but these words seemed to them an idle tale" (Luke 24:11).

24. N. T. Wright, in his excellent book *The Resurrection of the Son of God*, examines a massive amount of evidence from the ancient world and comes to a definitive conclusion: while many nations and individuals had well-developed ideas of the afterlife, that afterlife was never seen as something corporeal. Christianity, with its emphasis on the resurrection of the flesh, is truly unique.

When we preach the good news of Jesus's death and resurrection, we create liminal space for our listeners – like Mary Magdalene did for the other disciples. God acts in that space, although in ways we cannot control or predict. In this liminal situation – "already, but not yet" – the future invades the present. Our hope for the glory to come transforms our perception of the present circumstances, and we begin to see glimpses of that future glory here and now.

Summary

Jesus's faithful followers are separated from "the world" through their new birth, which means, among other things, that they are no longer blind. They are given an ability to interpret reality in a meaningful and empowering way. They have a new understanding of glory and shame. What used to be shameful – excommunication from the synagogue and other forms of ostracism – now becomes glorious. The supreme example of this transformation is their understanding of Jesus's death as the way of return to God's glory.

In the OT, the word translated "lift up" could mean both glorification and ultimate shame. So, in the NT, Jesus's death has two very different meanings: "the world" sees it as a defeat, the faithful disciples see it as a glorious victory. This difference in understanding the cross contributes greatly to the disciples' separation from "the world." If they have this second view of the crucifixion, they do not need to be physically removed from "the world" – they will be "not of the world" wherever they are.

Disciples rejoice at the memory of Jesus's resurrection and at the prospect of their own resurrection in glory. Resurrection becomes for them a vantage point from which they can interpret events in the life of Jesus and in their own lives. John shares with his readers this privileged post-resurrection perspective. One of the benefits of this glorious vision is a holistic understanding of Scripture.

When Jesus sends his disciples into the world, he does not promise physical safety – quite the opposite (15:18; 21:18–19). But Jesus knows that the world will not be able to destroy the new identity he has given his disciples. One of the ways in which this identity is safeguarded is through a radically different interpretation of the OT. This kind of interpretation was absent in post-AD 70 mainstream Judaism and, in the long run, is incompatible with how most rabbis in John's day interpreted the Hebrew Bible. Disciples of Jesus may be relatively few in number, they may suffer expulsion from synagogues and other forms of persecution, but it is they, and not their opponents, who have a consistent interpretation of the OT and the history of their own people. That history is not a tragedy but the story of God conquering the world through Jesus.

Disciples who hold to this understanding of Scripture – not as a book of rules but as a book of fulfilled promises – will become more competent interpreters of their own lives, even if those lives are torn by the sin of the world. One of the most fascinating discoveries they can make has to do with liminality – the "already, but not yet" situation created by Jesus's resurrection and a faithful Scripture-based testimony about it. We find ourselves in this liminality, and we create it for other people when we witness to the torn world.

Part II

"In the World"

5

Two Kinds of Glory

In the previous chapters, we saw how Jesus separates his followers from the world. He gives them a new identity – based on their new birth in Spirit – and eternal life in his kingdom. This new birth and adoption are accompanied by great privileges, including the ability to see God's glory and to have a coherent messianic interpretation of the OT Scriptures. These aspects of the disciples' identity alienate them from their own people and, since disciples are to live and witness among these people, further conflict is inevitable. Jesus heals his followers who are traumatized by persecution and then sends them back to the world, where they will face even more persecution.

The new birth received, the gift of the Spirit, and the disciples' new understanding of the OT Scripture and Jesus's death cannot be taken away by the world. But these blessings are bound to lead to an even greater conflict since the children of God will never be quite at home with "children of the devil" who persecute the church. Those who understand the OT as a book of messianic promises fulfilled in Jesus will not be content with the legalistic interpretation of the Scriptures. Those who see God's glory in the seemingly shameful suffering of Jesus will not always be welcomed by those who seek glory elsewhere. For John, this gap between two kinds of glory is at the root of many conflicts described in his gospel.

This chapter will be dedicated to the difference between God's glory and its substitute. The eyes that see God's glory on the cross of Christ will probably also see this glory in other unexpected contexts such as in the battered community of frightened disciples. But they are also likely to notice the absence of this glory in places and situations where it could be expected – for example, in religious circles where God's law is given lip service. A new understanding of glory also implies a new understanding of shame.

Where Does God's Glory Dwell?
Tabernacle, Temple, Flesh

In the prologue, John mentions that Jesus was rejected by "his own" (1:11). Then, in the next two verses, the Evangelist describes the essence of the new community Jesus created – the family of God's children who have experienced new birth (1:12–13). In the verse that follows, John speaks about one of the greatest privileges of these children of God – they are able to see God's glory (1:14). This glory is closely connected with the incarnation of the Son of God. These three themes – rejection by one's own, a new identity through new birth, and seeing God's glory – are united by one great overarching theme: incarnation and temple Christology. As John begins to develop this theme, he uses an important term that is not always translated accurately: "And the Word became flesh and dwelt among us, and we have seen his glory, glory as of the only Son from the Father, full of grace and truth" (1:14). The word translated as "dwelt" (ἐσκήνωσεν, *eskenosen*)[1] is derived from the noun σκηνή (*skene*) – literally, "tent" (as, for example, in Matt 17:4).[2] In the NT, however, this noun usually refers to the tabernacle – the portable sanctuary built at Sinai after the exodus.[3]

This tent travelled with the Israelites throughout their time of desert wandering and was the centre of their worship for several centuries after Israel conquered the promised land. During the reign of David, religion in Israel was centralized in Jerusalem. David's son Solomon built a magnificent temple that replaced the portable σκηνή (*skene*) as the place of worship.[4] That temple was destroyed by Babylonian invaders around 586 BC – a catastrophe that created shock waves, as reflected in many OT passages. When the Babylonian captivity ended, the Jews were allowed to return to Jerusalem and rebuild the temple. The six-hundred-year history of that restored temple was also marked by struggle. In the second century BC, the temple was defiled by Gentiles, then cleansed by the Maccabees, and the last hundred years of its existence was a time of continual renovation. Rulers of the Herodian dynasty, although cruel and godless tyrants, loved to adorn the temple, and so, by the time of Jesus, it was possible to exclaim, "Look . . . what wonderful stones and what wonderful

---

1. The dictionary form is σκηνόω.

2. Thus, the apostle Paul made his living as σκηνοποιός (*skenopoios*), a tentmaker (Acts 18:3).

3. See Acts 7:44; Hebrews 9:21.

4. Although some biblical authors, emphasizing continuity between the tabernacle in the desert and the temple in Jerusalem (and the temple of Jesus's resurrected body), use the term σκηνή for both (see Heb 13:10).

buildings!" (Mark 13:1) and to note that "it has taken forty-six years to build this temple" (John 2:20).

Shortly after the renovation was finished, the Jewish War broke out. In AD 70, Roman legions besieged Jerusalem and burned the temple.[5] Once again, Israel found itself scattered among the nations, seemingly deprived of a sanctuary. It is in this historical context that John uses the word "dwelt" (ἐσκήνωσεν, *eskenosen*) indicating that there is a connection between Jesus's body and Israel's tabernacle (σκηνή, *skene*).

But before discussing this connection, it might be useful to give a brief overview of the history of Israel's dealing with the tabernacle. It is a history of a torn nation trying to live with a torn sanctuary. It is a history of God's glory but also of Israel's defeat and shame – shame experienced but, fortunately, overcome.

When God called Israel out of Egypt, he explained why he wanted his people to be free: "Let my people go, that they may serve me" (Exod 9:1).[6] Israel was called to be God's "treasured possession among all peoples . . . a kingdom of priests and a holy nation" (Exod 19:5–6). When God gave the Israelites their unique identity, he promised, "I will make my dwelling among you, and my soul shall not abhor you. And I will walk among you and will be your God, and you shall be my people" (Lev 26:11–12). This promise indicates restoration – at least to some degree – of what was lost in Eden, where God is portrayed as "walking" among human beings (Gen 3:8).

When the tabernacle was erected in the midst of the Israelites' camp, the promise began to be fulfilled. Yet, from the beginning, it became obvious that God's holy dwelling in the midst of sinful Israel would be a source of ongoing conflict. Even before the tabernacle was built, Israel rebelled against God:

> They made a calf in Horeb
>   and worshipped a metal image.
> They exchanged the glory of God
>   for the image of an ox that eats grass. (Ps 106:19–20)

---

5. Some of the profits derived from plundering the immense temple treasury were used to build the Flavian Amphitheatre in Rome – named after the new dynasty whose first representatives, Vespasian and Titus, asserted themselves by ruthlessly suppressing the Jewish revolt. Today that theatre is better known by its popular name: Colosseum.

6. This powerful phrase has reverberated through the centuries, inspiring many courageous people to resist oppression and tyranny. In twenty-first-century Ukraine, this phrase is often used to express the independent nation's longing to be free from the Russian Empire (or what is left of it). Yet, often, a truncated version of the quotation is used, and the second part – "that they may serve me" – does not always get the attention it deserves. The Bible does not treat political freedom as the ultimate goal but only as the means to man's chief end, which is to glorify God.

This tendency to exchange God's glory for something pathetically worthless was present in Israel throughout its history and, arguably – as I will discuss in the next section of this chapter – culminated with the coming of Jesus when many of "his own" exchanged God's glory for a cheap substitute.

In the book of Exodus, the conflict was temporarily resolved through Moses's intercession. The book ends on a triumphant note, with God's glory filling the tabernacle (Exod 40:34–35). But it is clear that God's dwelling in the midst of sinful people would often cause the people much discomfort.

The laws given in the book of Leviticus were intended to protect God's holiness from the uncleanness of Israel. The annual Day of Atonement can be viewed as a ritual cleansing of the tabernacle that was defiled by daily contact with people who often failed to keep themselves pure. These laws also protected the people from God's holiness, and passages such as Leviticus 10:1–2 (where Nadab and Abihu die) show that this protection was necessary.

In the centuries following Israel's conquest of the promised land, there were also some dark chapters in the history of the people's dealing with the sanctuary. Towards the end of the period of the Judges, both the worship and worshippers were so badly abused by worthless priests that God allowed the tabernacle to be plundered by the Philistines and the ark of the covenant – its most important part – to be taken into captivity (1 Sam 4:11).

When Israel lived without the ark (and without a functioning tabernacle), it was truly a torn people, unable to fulfil its high calling. From a human perspective, it might seem that the history of Israel's dealing with God's tabernacle was over, ending in a most shameful way. But God resolved that crisis in a most unexpected manner, and God's dealings with Israel continued.

When the ark of the covenant was taken into captivity, this event foreshadowed the future captivity of the whole nation of Israel. The ark, in spite of being violated and defiled, revealed God's glory to the Gentiles. Through the ark, God showed his superiority over the gods of the Philistines (1 Samuel 5). These Gentiles feared his anger, and they even made sacrifices to try to appease him (1 Sam 6:3). Ultimately, they let the ark go, and God's people were given another opportunity to worship him properly.

When the ark was captured, Eli's daughter-in-law named her newborn son "Ichabod" – which means "without glory" – because, as she explained, "glory has departed from Israel, for the ark of God has been captured" (1 Sam 4:21–22). But when, through God's supernatural intervention, the ark was returned, the story of the ark's exile became a story of God's glory among the Gentiles.

When Solomon's Temple was destroyed and God's people went into exile, their story resembled the story of the ark and the Philistines. They experienced great shame, and it looked like their unique status among the nations was lost forever since there was nothing kingly or priestly about these humiliated prisoners of war. But God restored them, and they – like the ark of the covenant – returned to Jerusalem; and there they began building the temple, which would surpass the previous temple in its glory (Hag 2:9). Although this restoration was financed largely by the Gentiles and their new king Cyrus, Scripture leaves us in no doubt that it was God's doing all along (Isa 45:1ff.).

Although the ark itself was lost by the time of the return from the Babylonian captivity, the parallel holds – God's people are seen as the most valuable part of the tabernacle or temple. That theological observation helps to explain the seeming discrepancy between Jeremiah's prophecy and the chronology of the temple. Although Jeremiah predicted that the Babylonian captivity would last for seventy years (Jer 25:11–12), in fact, only about fifty years passed between the destruction of the temple (586 BC) and the fall of Babylon, with Cyrus's decree marking the beginning of the restoration (538 BC).

Daniel knew Jeremiah's prophecy, and he found the solution for this chronological difficulty (Dan 9:1–2): the destruction of the temple was not the beginning of the Babylonian captivity. The exile began with a deportation of Jews about twenty years before the fall of Jerusalem. Daniel himself was among the deportees, and he mentions that the Babylonians also took "some of the vessels of the house of God" (Dan 1:2).

Those vessels would play an important role in Babylon's fall – when King Belshazzar decided to profane these vessels (Dan 5:2–4), that very moment marked the end of his reign. When the God of Israel was insulted in such a high-handed way, he showed his power. Yet, throughout the book of Daniel, one gets the impression that the vessels of the temple were something more than just gold and silver cups. People like Daniel were God's real treasure among the nations – his faithful remnant.[7] Through them and their courageous testimony, God's name was greatly magnified among the Gentiles.

The exile of God's people was also the exile of God's temple treasure and the exile of his glory. The prophet Ezekiel saw God's glory departing from the temple and moving in an eastward direction (Ezek 10:18–19). It is not that the cloud of glory travelled all the way to Babylon, but Ezekiel does show

---

7. This idea – that God's most valued possession is people – was already present in the OT (Deut 32:10). It was developed by postexilic prophets (Zech 2:8) and affirmed in the NT (1 Pet 2:9). When God speaks about his chosen vessel Saul (Paul), he also mentions this vessel's mission among the Gentiles (Acts 9:15).

a connection between the captivity of God's people and the movement of God's glory.

In the Bible, going east often has an ominous meaning. When Adam and Eve were exiled from the garden, they went east (Gen 3:24). When Cain was exiled from God's presence, he went to a land "east of Eden" (4:16). After the flood, when people went east and stopped at a plain in the land of Shinar (11:2), the reader can expect that something bad would soon happen – and indeed, they started building the Tower of Babel. This eastward movement is often laden with ominous symbolism, and Israel's enemies often came from the east. The greatest catastrophe in the history of OT Israel involved a long journey eastward – to Babylon.

But as Isaiah and other OT prophets explain, this exile was part of God's plan to restore Israel (Isa 6:11–13). When the exiles returned to Judea, they struggled to be faithful to God in many areas of their lives,[8] but they no longer worshipped Baal and other false gods. While the spiritual life of the restored community was still far from perfect, having learned the painful lesson of the Babylonian captivity, they no longer made molten images and engaged in other idolatrous practices in the temple. Catastrophic as it was, the exile resulted in a spiritual renewal of God's people.

In the OT prophetic books, God is not unlike a doctor who performs an extremely painful surgery – the kind of operation no one else can do – which results in a new quality of life for the patient. When the exiles gathered for departure, their grief was indescribable: "Rachel is weeping for her children; she refuses to be comforted" (Jer 31:15). But those deportees who believed the words of Isaiah and Jeremiah probably understood that this long journey east was part of Israel's restoration. Some of them, or their children and grandchildren, would eventually go west – they would return to serve the Lord in a way that would glorify him. In chapter 3 (see section titled "Jesus's Death: Not a Tragedy"), we had an example in which going east eventually meant going west. In that example, this was possible because of the travellers' persistence. Here, the change becomes possible through the Israelites' repentance.

God cleansed Jerusalem through the literal fire of the Babylonian invasion and through the metaphorical fire of the exile. He did this for his glory because his people needed to have genuine faith to serve him as they ought to. Just like precious metals are put through fire to be refined, the faithful remnant – God's true treasure among the nations – was put through the crucible of the exile.

---

8. Haggai 1:9; Malachi 1:6–8.

Two Kinds of Glory 89

A similar pattern can be discerned in the NT. Jesus predicted the destruction of the temple, but that destruction did not mean the end of God's dealings with his people. The destruction of the tabernacle and the captivity of the ark brought glory to the God of Israel. The destruction of the First Temple and the captivity of God's faithful people eventually brought glory to the God of Israel. The destruction of the Second Temple, which was followed by the scattering of God's people all over the world, will also bring glory to the God of Israel.

After AD 70, both the tabernacle and its people would go into a painful and glorious exile. In his body, this new tabernacle, Jesus wandered (ἐσκήνωσεν, *eskenosen*) with his people; and he continues to do so for, even now, he wanders with us through the desert of this world.

Ukrainian Christians scattered throughout the world may also see themselves as God's vessels who, paradoxically, happen to be in places where they do not belong but where God wants them to be. When we come to grips with this paradox, we join the countless multitude of believers throughout the ages who had to learn to serve God in adverse and seemingly chaotic circumstances.

> The Christian cannot simply take for granted the privilege of living among other Christians. Jesus Christ lived in the midst of his enemies. In the end all his disciples abandoned him. On the cross he was all alone, surrounded by criminals and the jeering crowds. He had come for the express purpose of bringing peace to the enemies of God. So Christians, too, belong not in the seclusion of a cloistered life but in the midst of enemies. There they find their mission, their work . . .
>
> "Though I scattered them among the nations, yet in far countries they shall remember me" (Zech 10:9). According to God's will, the Christian church is a scattered people, scattered like seed "to all the kingdoms of the earth" (Deut 28:25). That is the curse and its promise. God's people must live in distant lands among the unbelievers, but they will be the seed of the kingdom of God in all the world.[9]

These words were written by a German theologian and pastor at a time when it was illegal for Christians to gather unless they agreed with the idolatrous oppressive regime. Many of Bonhoeffer's colleagues experienced

---

9. Bonhoeffer, *Life Together*, 1–2.

exile without even leaving their homeland. Like Jesus, they became aliens in their own country, among their "own" people. Bonhoeffer's insights remind us that while this situation is, of course, abnormal, it is not unusual if viewed against the background of the history of the church, beginning with OT times.

Abnormal, but not unusual. This paradox was present in the life of Jesus who offered hospitality to people (Matt 11:28–30) while he himself had nowhere to lay his head (Matt 8:20). For many Ukrainian Christians (including myself), separation from the home church is one of the most painful aspects of the exile. When we are physically separated from the church, we do not stop being part of the church, and – another paradox – being part of the church may include separation from the community where we feel we belong. As we wander through the desert of this world, Jesus wanders with us.

At this point, one may ask this question: How can Jesus be present among his people now if he ascended to heaven almost two thousand years ago? To answer this question, we need to look at another aspect of John's temple Christology – continuity between the sanctuaries of Israel.

Continuity and Fullness

Many people, when asked about the purpose of the tabernacle in the OT, would answer that it was a temporary structure that provided the Israelites with an opportunity to worship God until the temple was built. That understanding of the tabernacle is not wrong. Both King David (Ps 132:1–5) and King Solomon (1 Kgs 8:13) seemed to have a similar view. But John's approach is different. For John, the temple in Jerusalem was a temporary arrangement, but, in the NT, the tabernacle is not something but, rather, someone who will last forever. Thus, in the new Jerusalem, there will be no temple as such (Rev 21:22). Neither God nor his worshippers will need a static sanctuary because there will be a movable, walking sanctuary: "Behold, the dwelling place [σκηνή, *skene*] of God is with man. He will dwell [σκηνώσει, *skenosei*] with them, and they will be his people, and God himself will be with them as their God" (Rev 21:3).

In Jesus, God dwelt with people. And in Jesus, he will dwell with people, fulfilling the great promise of Leviticus 26:11–12. We live in the time between the two instalments of the fulfilment of that promise. We live in a liminality – in the "already, but not yet" state that was explained in chapter 4. Studying the connection between God's sanctuaries in history may help us discover an aspect that strengthens the "already" part of that perception of reality. There is much there to observe for eyes that see God's glory.

Transition from one type of sanctuary to another was never painless. When, under King David, the Israelites tried to bring the ark of the covenant into its new resting place, one of them died because he failed to treat God's glory with proper respect (2 Sam 6:6–7). Destruction of the First Temple was accompanied by an enormous death toll, and a prerequisite for the construction of the Second Temple was the downfall of the Babylonian Empire. When the Second Temple was burned in AD 70, it was a catastrophic military and spiritual defeat for Israel.

John helps his readers to turn from the temple made by human hands to the temple of Jesus's resurrected body. But that transition was only possible because Jesus was ready to suffer the horrific violence described in the passion narrative.[10] And of course, the final establishment of God's kingdom on earth is described as being accompanied by destruction on a cosmic scale.

Since discontinuity is clearly present in all the transitions from one type of sanctuary to another, it is easy to lose sight of continuity. But continuity is crucial for John's theology of the temple. For example, when Jesus cleansed the temple, he told his opponents, "Destroy this temple, and in three days I will raise it up" (2:19). He did not say, "I will raise another temple in its stead." His resurrection did not produce a new temple but, rather, restores an already existing one.

In OT theology, the temple is a place – or rather, *the* place – where God's glory dwelt in a special way. God knows that we are physical beings who are limited by time and space. We cannot be in more than one location at the same time. When we choose to be present in one place, that automatically excludes all others. When God deals with us, he is mindful of these limitations. Although he is omnipresent, he gave the Israelites a limited sacred space where his presence was revealed in a special way. As he announced to Solomon, "I have consecrated this house that you have built, by putting my name there for ever. My eyes and my heart will be there for all time" (1 Kgs 9:3).

God put his holy "heart" in this place in the midst of the sinful Israelites. This meant that he made himself vulnerable – to the extent that this word can be applied to God. His name and, thus, his glory could be – and, unfortunately, was – profaned by Israel's sins. But God knows what he is doing, and he will bring the world to the state in which the redeemed can rejoice in his presence and see his glory. He will overcome the world.

---

10. The Evangelist also shows that switching from a synagogue-based liturgy to Jesus-centred worship was a traumatic experience for many.

In John, the Jerusalem Temple is a temporary structure that anticipated the coming of the tabernacle of Jesus's body. Or, to continue using Menken's metaphor, much of what was going on in the temple was a form waiting to be filled with a new meaning. Jesus fulfilled the theology of the temple because many of the promises usually associated with the temple were fulfilled in him. For John, the tabernacle of Jesus's body is not a new temple replacing the old one; it is the old temple fulfilled.

This observation prepares us to deal with another question: How many temples was Jesus talking about in John 2:19 – one or two? My answer would be that Jesus's words can be understood on two levels. On one level, he spoke about two different temples. Both those temples would be destroyed – his own body would be crucified at the end of his ministry, and the edifice in Jerusalem would be destroyed in AD 70. The destruction of those two temples were two separate events. On another level, Jesus spoke about one temple. His resurrection from the dead was this one temple being restored. The stone edifice did not need to be rebuilt, but the resurrection of Jesus's body *is* restoring the Jerusalem Temple and all the hopes ever associated with it.

If we follow this interpretation, we come to a chronological anomaly. After Jesus was raised from the dead, the temple was already restored but not yet destroyed. How could this be? One possible way of dealing with this difficulty[11] is to distinguish between two concepts: the temple as a stone structure and the temple as a place where God's glory dwells. When the leaders of Israel put Jesus to death, they destroyed his body, but they also destroyed the temple as the place of God's glory. The stone edifice remained for another forty years, but its meaning changed. From that time on, God's glory would dwell elsewhere.

This interpretation also helps make sense of God's promise in 1 Kings 9:3. God's name would be on his house "forever," but, as Peter explains, God's house is more, much more, than just a stone building (1 Pet 2:5). When God allowed the Jerusalem Temple to be destroyed, his promise did not fail. God's unexpected way of fulfilling his promise is quite in line with the play on words used in 2 Samuel 7: David wanted to build a house for God, but God had a better offer – he would build a house for David (2 Sam 7:11). The word translated as "house" can mean both a building and a dynasty.

The fullness of God's glory, the fullness of what a human being can ever see of God, abides in Jesus. Whoever has seen Jesus has seen the Father (John

---

11. I realize, of course, that some readers will be perfectly content to live with this anomaly. John's gospel is full of liminalities, and this is just one of those instances where the future invades the present, as is typical given John's realized eschatology.

14:9). Jesus's body is where the fullness of God's presence is to be found. He is the new tabernacle who dwelt among the rebellious Israelites. When Jesus was crucified, that tabernacle was destroyed. When he rose from the dead, it was rebuilt; or, to be more precise, the rebuilding process began – and still continues (Eph 2:21).

When the disciples first met Jesus and asked him where he was "staying" (John 1:38) – a form of the Greek verb μένω, *meno* – they probably could not have imagined what his answer would be. But as they progressed to a deeper understanding of Jesus's identity, they discovered that he desired to "abide" (μένω, *meno*) in them (15:4) and intended to make them parts of a living temple – the one that he restored on the third day.

To describe the experience of the disciples who "abide" (μένω, *meno*) in Jesus – and in whom he abides – even after his ascension, one can use two complementary concepts: union with Christ and communion with Christ. Union with Christ has to do with who we are – recipients of the new birth, God's children resurrected from spiritual death and given a new identity. Nothing can ever change that status (10:28). Our communion with Christ, on the other hand, is a dynamic reality, which includes our daily battles with sin – with their victories and defeats – and a quest for God's glory. This communion can be strengthened or weakened; it can be deepened or made superficial. In this fallen world, this communion will never be perfect, but we are promised a gift of perfection in the age to come (Heb 12:23).

Thus, in some sense, born-again Christians "abide" in Christ no matter what they do; and in some other sense, they have to strive to "abide" in him. John's gospel also encourages readers to "abide" in Jesus's word (8:31–32) and in his love (15:9). They are called to live according to who they are – God's living temple.

John wrote his gospel at a time the Jewish community throughout the world was shaken by the aftermath of the AD 70 disaster. As Judaism reinvented itself, one of the main questions the survivors struggled with had to do with celebrating holidays. The law of Moses prescribed pilgrimages to Jerusalem and sacrificing in the tabernacle or temple. When such pilgrimages became impossible, various substitutes were offered – for example, visiting a famous teacher of the law. In John's gospel, this is what Nicodemus did when he came to Jesus around the time of Passover (2:13); and "a large crowd," fickle though it was, also came to Jesus in Galilee, far from Jerusalem, during Passover (6:1–4).

Is there a special place on earth where God's presence can be experienced even after the destruction of the temple in Jerusalem? Yes; it is in the gathering of Jesus's disciples. A member of such a community can say, "It is no longer I who live, but Christ who lives in me" (Gal 2:20). This is God's tabernacle that has been taken into exile. Jesus sends his disciples into the world, where they will experience rejection and shame. Yet, it is through these disciples and their courageous testimony that God's name will be glorified among the nations.

The apostle Peter describes his fellow disciples as "living stones . . . being built up as a spiritual house" of God (1 Pet 2:5). In the same verse, he also calls them "a holy priesthood" because they serve in the temple of Jesus's resurrected body. But disciples of Jesus can also be compared to the vessels of the temple – although taken far away into a foreign land and treated with contempt, they will bring glory to God. The path to God's greater glory is through suffering and humiliation. The road leading up goes down. The disciples are torn people sent into the torn world, but they will overcome the world if they live for God's glory.

The Glory That Comes from People

In the first chapter of his gospel, John makes it clear that Jesus has supernatural access to information about other people. Jesus "saw" Nathanael under a fig tree in a location physically removed from where they met (1:48). The rest of the narrative provides many other examples. Jesus knew about Lazarus's death that took place far away. Not only did he acquire information about people and places in a supernatural way, he miraculously influenced the course of events from a distance (see John 4:50–53).[12] After his resurrection, when the disciples spent a whole night fishing, Jesus knew exactly where they would be in the morning and made sure there was an enormous amount of fish right there.

Jesus knows about people's past (4:17–18) and future – both near (13:37–38) and distant (21:18–19). He also knows their hearts and perceives secret desires and motivations that they themselves might not even be aware of (2:24–25; 6:15, 26). This kind of knowledge sometimes creates awkward and ironic situations. When the disciples had just begun following Jesus, they knew very little about him, but they also knew very little about themselves and about their own motives and expectations. This tension is also present in the lives of disciples who cannot follow Jesus physically on the roads of first-century Palestine but do follow him spiritually. We follow the one who knows us better than we know ourselves.

---

12. Knowledge of this detail places the careful reader in a privileged position. When Martha says, "Lord, if you had been here, my brother would not have died" (11:21), we already know – from John 4:50–53 – that Jesus did not need to be physically present with Lazarus to prevent his death. He chose not to heal Lazarus so that he could resurrect him and reveal God's glory in a very special way.

What does Jesus see when he looks into people's hearts? He sees creatures made in God's image and created to bring glory to God. Unfortunately, the fall mutilated the hearts of those creatures; now, they still seek glory but, since they consider themselves some sort of divine beings, at the centre of their universe, they seek glory for themselves. For John, this is the essence of sin. While sometimes using the plural form "sins" (as in 8:24), he often speaks about "the sin" of the world (1:29). Although John does not specify what exactly that sin is, in the context of the whole Gospel, it is quite clear that "the sin of the world" has to do with striving for autonomy – that is, the world's desire to live without God (3:19).

Every sin is ugly, but some medieval theologians taught that pride is the mother of all sins. Perhaps John would agree with them to some extent. When people's hearts are set on getting glory for themselves, even a good thing like the word of God may be abused. This was the problem with the Pharisees and scribes who debated with Jesus. They read the Scriptures, but, because their hearts were set on glorifying themselves, they used the Scriptures as a means of self-advancement: "How can you believe, when you receive glory from one another and do not seek the glory that comes from the only God?" (5:44).

This search for one's own glory may take a variety of forms, which can be divided into two general categories: arrogance and people-pleasing.

Arrogance

Arrogance or hubris is an attitude that reflects a person's belief in their own superiority. This perceived superiority is understood as either inherent (resulting from one's birth in the right family) or achieved (resulting from one's success in some kind of competition). In the Gospel of John, the rulers and teachers of Israel are portrayed as having this kind of overbearing attitude towards their fellow Jews, including Jesus.

C. S. Lewis considers this kind of pride the worst sin and notes, sadly, that this sin can be found among religious people as well:

> Other vices may sometimes bring people together: you may find good fellowship and jokes and friendliness among drunken people or unchaste people. But pride always means enmity – it is enmity. And not only enmity between man and man, but enmity to God.
>
> In God you come up against something which is in every respect immeasurably superior to yourself. Unless you know God as that – and, therefore, know yourself as nothing in comparison –

you do not know God at all. As long as you are proud you cannot know God. A proud man is always looking down on things and people: and, of course, as long as you are looking down, you cannot see something that is above you.

That raises a terrible question. How is it that people who are quite obviously eaten up with Pride can say they believe in God and appear to themselves very religious? I am afraid it means they are worshipping an imaginary God. They theoretically admit themselves to be nothing in the presence of this phantom God, but are really all the time imagining how He approves of them and thinks them far better than ordinary people: that is, they pay a pennyworth of imaginary humility to Him and get out of it a pound's worth of Pride towards their fellow-men.[13]

The Gospel of John is full of examples of such people who keep looking down on other human beings, even their own colleagues who notice their prejudice (7:50–52).

When Jesus, in his great humility, entered their social space, they looked down on him, too. Then something truly terrible happened – they become blind. John wanted his readers to see this blindness as a sign of judgement. In John's realized eschatology, anticipation of judgement is part of the judgement itself.

One can draw an analogy with the OT story of the two angels who visited Sodom (Gen 19:1–29). The angels, who were messengers of God, had been sent to participate in judging this city – to investigate and establish whether the accusations against it were true. The inhabitants of the city did not understand that they were being judged, and they tried to abuse the investigators. The narrator's scathing irony is shown in various ways, including the comment made by the people of Sodom. When Lot tried to intervene, they yelled at him: "This fellow came to sojourn, and he has become the judge!" (Gen 19:9) – when it is actually the visitors they seek to abuse who are their judge.

The people of Sodom were trying to commit an abominable sin. In addition, they were hypersensitive to any sign of disapproval and viewed even Lot's feeble attempt to intervene as being judgemental. Anything remotely resembling "judgement" – even Lot's humble pleading – made them furious; but they seemed oblivious to the true and severe judgement that was about to come upon them.

---

13. Lewis, *Mere Christianity*, 124.

God's messengers blinded the men of Sodom, and that blinding was a sign anticipating the judgement that would come just a few hours later. In one sense, their blindness was a sign of the judgement being carried out "here and now"; in another sense, it was a sign of the judgement that would soon come. Blinded by God's messengers, the wicked groped in the dark as they awaited the final judgement[14] that would fall upon them. They were in a liminal state of judgement – "already, but not yet" – already judged but not yet given the full measure of that judgement.

This OT background helps us understand what happened to the arrogant leaders of Israel in the Gospel of John. Jesus himself explained it this way: "For judgement I came into this world, that those who do not see may see, and those who see may become blind" (John 9:39). The leaders of Israel are depicted as blind – incapable of seeing even the simplest cause-and-effect connections in many events in the Gospel – and this blindness seems to go from bad to worse. After interacting with Jesus, they become even more hardened towards the truth and even more hostile towards those who witnessed to this truth.

When Jesus blinded the arrogant religious leaders, he was following the pattern established in the OT. He continued doing what Isaiah and other prophets had done (Isa 6:10). And followers of Jesus will also follow this pattern: they will blind the opponents of the gospel, sometimes physically (as in Acts 13:9–11) but most often spiritually.

Arrogant religious leaders who seek glory for themselves totally fail to see the glory of God, even when confronted with extraordinary supernatural signs. But arrogance is not the only way in which the glory that comes from people can be sought. In his gospel, John shows another way people may seek this vain glory. That way is not so conspicuous, but it can be just as deadly. This second way is people-pleasing, and the Fourth Gospel has much to say about this.

People-Pleasing

When the Fourth Evangelist portrays the Pharisees and other religious authorities as arrogant and self-seeking, his descriptions are not greatly different from those we find in the Synoptic Gospels. In Matthew, for example, Jesus noted that the scribes and Pharisees liked receiving signs of respect: "They love the place of honour at feasts and the best seats in the synagogues

---

14. This judgement with fire and brimstone is "final" only in the immediate context of the book of Genesis. As the words of Jesus in Matthew 11:23–24 indicate, the final judgement for Sodom and Gomorrah is still to come.

and greetings in the market-places and being called rabbi by others" (Matt 23:6–7). John's complementary approach is interesting because, among other things, he places additional emphasis on the Pharisees' attitude to the common people. We know from the Synoptics that the scribes and Pharisees loved being glorified through visible signs of respect such as greetings and special seats. But what did they say (among themselves) about the people who showed them such honour? Did they believe that respect is a two-way street? No, they did not.

In the Gospel of John, the Pharisees and other religious leaders showed contempt towards the common people who held them in high regard. For example, they described the pilgrims gathered for the Feast of Booths as "this crowd that does not know the law [and] is accursed" (John 7:49). In the OT, a pagan king offered great riches to Balaam (a seer) in exchange for cursing Israel. Balaam refused (Num 22:18), even though his love for money was great. But in the Gospel of John, we see leaders of Israel who do not even need an incentive to curse their own people, and their offhanded remark implies that they did this habitually, without much thought.

The scribes' responsibility was to teach the people. If the people did not know the law, this was also the fault of these scribes. But they were obsessed with seeking glory from one another (5:44), and their study of the law had become for them nothing more than a way of self-aggrandizing. They were shepherds who were feeding themselves (Ezek 34:2–6). The irony is heightened by the fact that this conversation took place during the Feast of Booths (John 7:2). A tradition going all the way back to the time of Ezra prescribed that this celebration be filled with teaching activities (Neh 8:1–8, 13–18). Yet, instead of teaching the people – many of whom had come from far away to worship God – the leaders treated them with contempt. It was Jesus, not the scribes, who taught during the feast (John 7:14).

The contrast between Jesus and the religious leaders of Israel could not be starker. Yet, many people in the Gospel of John are shown as choosing those leaders over Jesus. Why did they make this choice? What makes sheep follow shepherds who only feed themselves?

> Therefore they could not believe. For again Isaiah said,
>
> "He has blinded their eyes
>   and hardened their heart,
> lest they see with their eyes,
>   and understand with their heart, and turn,
>   and I would heal them."

> Isaiah said these things because he saw his glory and spoke of him. Nevertheless, many even of the authorities believed in him, but for fear of the Pharisees they did not confess it, so that they would not be put out of the synagogue; for they loved the glory that comes from man more than the glory that comes from God. (John 12:39–43)

In the previous section, I discussed the judicial blinding of Israel's leaders – that is, an act of judgement that functions as a sign of future judgement. But those leaders were not the only ones who experienced blindness. Many common people also fell into this category. They also failed to give glory to God – that is, they failed to accept the one sent by God – because, according to John, they "loved the glory that comes from man." What is that "glory"?

In this particular context, "the glory that comes from man" was nothing more than just keeping their membership in the synagogue. Of course, losing that membership could mean severe psychological suffering and, as explained in chapter 1 (see section titled "'The World' in the Gospel of John"), often led to physical violence. Those who chose to avoid that kind of suffering protected themselves from shame – but was that absence of shame equal to receiving glory?

This is a passage where John's irony is breathtaking in its scope. Keeping one's membership in the synagogue could be associated with some kind of "glory" since it meant avoiding much shame. The word "glory" is used here to indicate a person's reputation or good standing in the community. But John contrasts this with another meaning of the word "glory" – God's glory[15] as it was revealed to Isaiah. Those who chose to avoid a conflict with the Pharisees missed that eternal glory. And, since being deprived of glory means shame, missing that eternal, infinite, perfect glory means eternal, infinite, unmitigated shame. We see here the paradox of the fallen world. When the world tries to flee judgement, it crawls deeper and deeper into darkness – and it is judged for that rejection of light.

John explains that the people who believed in Jesus but chose to remain in the synagogue were driven by fear – fear of the Pharisees and other authorities.

---

15. It is remarkable that the pronoun "his" in John 12:41 can be interpreted as referring to Christ. From a purely human perspective, this phrase might seem hopelessly anachronistic since Isaiah lived seven centuries before the incarnation of the Son of God. But the phrase makes perfect sense in the context of the Gospel of John, where Jesus referred to the glory he had with the Father even before the creation of the world (17:5).

Such fear makes people do cruel things – in this case, even refusing to support and protect their own children (see 9:22).

It is easy to draw moralistic conclusions: we should not fear people, but, instead, we should fear God; we should not be people-pleasers, but, instead, we should seek God's glory. But such simplistic conclusions are hard to put into practice. Humans are social beings. We were designed to live in fellowship not only with God but also with each other. Receiving messages of approval – both in verbal and non-verbal forms – is a legitimate need because that is how we have been created.

Jesus himself is aware of our need for affirmation and approval. In the Gospel of John, he communicated approval in many situations, sometimes unexpected ones. For example, he praised both Nathanael and the Samaritan woman for their honesty (1:47; 4:17–18). In his prayer to the Father, he affirmed his disciples' progress in faith (17:6–8) – which was generous praise considering that, in just a few hours, these disciples would all desert him.

Jesus encouraged his followers to abide in him, which means, among other things, receiving positive affirmation from him on a regular basis. Jesus can do this because he himself constantly receives approval from his Father. The three persons of the Trinity, who abide in perfect love, constantly send each other messages of love (although the word "messages" in this context is, of course, crudely anthropomorphic). From the very beginning, God's salvific plan was to include human beings in this eternal exchange of love.

Some religions – and some groups within Christianity – emphasize the false ideal of striving to live without the need for anyone's praise and approval. Fascinating as this suggestion may sound, it is not realistic because it does not take into account the psychological make-up of humans as created beings. The gospel teaches us to seek God's approval in everything we do. It also makes us aware of the conflict within our own hearts – the desire to seek God's glory often has to compete with the desire to receive approval from people.

Truly wise people know that they need the approval of significant others in their lives, but, because they are wise, they also know how to configure the system of those significant others. They know whose opinions are important, whose opinions are less important, and whose opinions are not important at all. A wise person's social world is not chaotic but structured. God is at the top of this structure. The wise seek God's approval in all things; and if something is not pleasing to God, they refuse to do it, even if "lesser players" in their social system would approve of such an action.

In the Gospel of John, the plight of those who chose the glory that comes from people over God's glory was the result of a false hierarchy. Close to the top of that hierarchy were the scribes and Pharisees – their opinions were regarded as ultimate verdicts. God, although given lip service, was removed from these people's model.

When considering practical and pastoral aspects, there is, of course, a great difference between people who sin because of their weakness and those who sin because of their wickedness. There is a great difference between the helpless sheep and their worthless shepherds. But when it comes to God's glory, the difference between these two kinds of sinners is not so pronounced. To those readers who hesitate to join the persecuted community of believers, John shows that the inability of the sheep to think for themselves is, in the long run, learned helplessness – which is something they will be held accountable for.

For Ukrainian Christians, this difference has far-reaching practical applications. One of the most challenging aspects of our situation is dealing with our enemies – the Russians who invaded our land, killing thousands of innocent people. What makes it harder is that some Russian and pro-Russian Christians ask us to work towards "reconciliation." Since this subject has caused much anger and controversy in some circles, one has to tread very carefully here. Yet, it is my belief that insights gained from reading the Gospel of John may help us take at least some steps towards solving this extremely complex problem.

One of the greatest obstacles towards a constructive dialogue between Ukrainian and Russian evangelicals is that the former usually completely reject the narratives created by Russian propaganda, whereas the latter often tend to accept these narratives, at least to some extent. Those narratives, bizarre as they are, blur the line between the aggressor and the victim – for instance, instead of aggression, one speaks about a "conflict" in which both sides share responsibility. From our (Ukrainian) perspective, this is unacceptable since there is a clear difference: Ukraine does not lay any claims to Russian territories, whereas Russia seeks to grab as much Ukrainian land as possible.

From a Christian point of view, there is a great difference in the area of religious freedom – in Ukraine, non-traditional (Protestant) denominations hardly ever experience government interference with their activities, whereas in Russia, evangelicals have very limited opportunities to practice and spread their faith. In the territories occupied by Russia, religious minorities suffer greatly, with believers arrested, beaten, and tortured, and church property confiscated or destroyed. We simply cannot accept a peace formula that fails to differentiate between the persecutors and the persecuted. This is why attempts at dialogue between Ukrainian and Russian Christians are often a fiasco.

Just a handful of Russian preachers and lay people have spoken openly against the aggressive war their country is waging. That is hardly surprising since Russian laws prescribe severe penalties for those who dare to criticize the government. There are, I hope, many Russian Christians who understand what their country is doing to the church in Ukraine, even though they keep their observations to themselves. I can understand them and even sympathize with them to some extent. They are not unlike John's secret believers – those who were attracted to the truth but afraid to lose their synagogue membership. Such believers do not want to be exposed to shame and threats to their safety.

Such Christians are weak – they lack courage and wisdom. But there is a great difference between them and those evangelicals who publicly support the Russian war efforts. Such church leaders, in my opinion, fall into a different category – those who seek glory for themselves. And in Russia, nowadays, this glory that comes from people – along with other privileges – is usually given to those who support the party line. The sin of these leaders is much graver, and there is no point seeking to be "reconciled" until they are ready to repent. And in order to repent, they would have to recognize that persecution of Christians in Russian-occupied territories of Ukraine is real and that they have aligned themselves with the persecutors.

This distinction between inadequate shepherds and their misled sheep may help Ukrainian Christians in the painful dialogue that will have to be resumed sooner or later. If we keep in mind the difference between those whose chief sin is people-pleasing because of fear and those whose chief sin is glory-seeking and arrogance, we may be able to avoid two extremes – being either unnecessarily harsh towards the weak or unreasonably lenient towards those who support persecution – in dealing with Russian Christians.

The disciple's quest for God's glory inevitably means a conflict with the world that seeks to glorify itself. The road leading to the heights of God's glory leads through a valley of humiliation. John encourages his readers not to be afraid of the contempt the world is going to pour on them. He teaches them to view expressions of this contempt – including various forms of psychological violence – not as obstacles to their discipleship but, rather, as part of it. The captured ark of the covenant brought glory to God when it was mistreated by the Philistines. The captured people of the covenant brought glory to God when they were mistreated by Babylonians. The temple of Jesus's body brought glory to God when it was being destroyed by Israel's false shepherds. The scattered people of the new covenant (including those who were put out of the synagogue) bring glory to God even, and perhaps especially, when they are persecuted. The next chapter contains a more detailed treatment of persecution and the disciples' mission.

Summary

The Gospel of John forms the identity of persecuted disciples by teaching them that God's glory abides with them and in them. This teaching was especially relevant in the post-AD 70 situation when the Jerusalem Temple was destroyed. Since the Jews believed that God's glory dwelt in that temple, after the fall of Jerusalem, access to God's glory became a painful subject for the survivors.

John shows that Jesus's resurrected body is the new temple where God dwells. This temple has some continuity with Israel's previous sanctuaries. Because Israel was a torn people, God's dwelling in their midst often involved some tension. The people did not always treat the sanctuary with respect, and God did not always shield them from the consequences of their sins.

The tabernacle, the first sanctuary of Israel, was captured by the Philistines but eventually returned, bringing glory to God. The First Temple was burned and its vessels taken into captivity. These vessels were also returned – along with a renewed and repentant people – bringing glory to God. The Second Temple was destroyed, but Jesus promised to restore the temple of his body. That renewed temple – the body in which Jesus "dwelt" among his people – was the fulfilment of many OT prophecies.

There is also continuity between the temple of Jesus's resurrected body and the church – which is the living temple of God's people. As the disciples worship God in and through this new temple, they experience his presence and bring glory to God. Their lives become a quest for God's glory, and John shows that one of their greatest challenges as they pursue this quest will be rejecting the lesser "glory that comes from man." In the Fourth Gospel, this rival glory takes two forms: arrogance (a feature characterizing many of the religious leaders of John's time) and people-pleasing – the sin of common people who are afraid of losing their social status. The former is worse, but, ultimately, both lead away from the true glory of God.

Being excommunicated from the synagogue meant losing the "glory that comes from man," but this was a necessary experience for at least some of those disciples who wanted to stay faithful to Jesus. While the Gospel of John does not deny the severity of such trauma, it teaches us to view such experiences as the result of a person's choice – the choice between God's eternal perfect glory and the temporary substitutes of people.

6

The Disciples' Path

The Gospel of John gives profound but paradoxical answers to some of the questions that form the core of our identity as human beings. John shows his persecuted readers that opposition, rejection, and suffering are part of God's glorious plan for saving the torn world. Jesus was glorified not just in spite of the cross but through the cross. His descent into the worst kind of shame was his ascent to the great glory of the Father. Not everyone is able to see that glory on the cross. But Jesus gives his followers new eyes, so to speak. His disciples – and John's readers – are enabled to see God's glory in what looks like total defeat to the world. This kind of vision comes with rejecting the "tragic" interpretation of Jesus's death and, by the same token, rejecting similar interpretations of the destruction of the temple. As discussed in the previous chapter, it was God's plan, right from the beginning, to glorify his name through his destroyed sanctuary. Let us look now at how similar interpretations apply to the life and death of Jesus's disciples – the individuals who make up his renewed temple.

Boundaries
"Us and Them"

In the prologue to his gospel, John states that Jesus "came to his own, and his own people did not receive him" (1:11). If John had stopped at this verse, this would have been the synopsis of a tragic story. But, in the verses that follow, John explains, "But to all who did receive him, who believed in his name, he gave the right to become children of God, who were born, not of blood nor of the will of the flesh nor of the will of man, but of God" (1:12–13).

Many interpreters would agree that the Gospel of John can be logically divided into two parts, with the second part beginning at 13:1. While Jesus's "own" are also mentioned in 13:1, these are not the same people who rejected him in 1:11. "Now before the Feast of the Passover, when Jesus knew that his hour had come to depart out of this world to the Father, having loved his own who were in the world, he loved them to the end" (13:1). It was the disciples – those who had believed in his word (17:6) – whom Jesus now considered "his own." But why does John say this here, rather than at the beginning of the gospel? He could have written something like this in his prologue:

> Jesus came to this world to save his own. He came to his own sheep, who listen to his voice. And he suffered at the hands of the people who never belonged to his sheep – people who were never his own, except for the few like Saul of Tarsus, who later repented.

None of these statements would be wrong, theologically. Yet, for John, it was important to emphasize that the rejection Jesus suffered from "his own" did not thwart God's plan. God's plan was fulfilled not just in spite of that rejection but through it.

As the disciples followed Jesus, they would also have to experience rejection from their "own" and be incorporated into a new group – the church as a community of love – that would now be identified as their "own."

In the context of reconstruction of the original Johannine community, as assumed by Martyn and those who follow his model, this means that Jewish believers in Jesus participated in the synagogue services and referred to other members of the synagogue as "we." After their excommunication, they began to refer to the synagogue community as "they." This would partially explain a strange feature of John where, when he talked about "the Jews," Jesus used third-person forms: "Little children, yet a little while I am with you. You will seek me, and just as I said to the Jews, so now I also say to you, 'Where I am going you cannot come'" (John 13:33). Jesus, himself a Jew, when he spoke to the disciples – who were all Jews – referred to "the Jews" as if he were speaking about some foreign nation.

Although there must have been other possible ways to refer to this group of people – for example, pilgrims in Jerusalem, worshippers in the temple, or the crowds who gathered to listen – John's irony makes it sound as though Jesus were referring to aliens of some kind. Since these people rejected him, he became a stranger to them (Ps 69:8) – but this also means that they became strangers to him and to his disciples. Soon, Jesus would send the disciples into the world – which included "the Jews" – and this sending would be in the way missionaries might be sent to foreign nations.

The language of "us" and "them" is a language of separation. It is about redrawing the boundaries so that some who used to belong to the "in" group will now be outsiders. One of the ways Jesus separates his disciples from the world is by teaching them to use the pronoun "they" in a different way. Once they are able to do this, he can send the disciples back to the world, confident that they will not lose the new identity he has given them. Thus, they will be able to interact with "the world" without being "conformed" to it (Rom 12:2).

Jesus teaches his followers to reject "tragic" interpretations of his death, and John shows that the cross was the path to glory. Similarly, Jesus teaches his disciples to reject "tragic" interpretations of their own life and death. He also teaches them to reject legalistic interpretations of the OT and embrace it as a book of God's promises fulfilled in Christ.

Jesus's words provide an interpretative framework – like a lens – that enables his disciples to see reality in a much clearer way. Disciples who see God's glory – and the fulfilment of OT prophecies – in Jesus's suffering will eventually begin to view their own experiences in a different way. Being "put out of the synagogue" or being rejected by family members and religious leaders is a traumatic experience. John the Evangelist does not deny that such experiences are painful, but he does provide an interpretative framework within which that rejection becomes a part of both the disciples' quest and God's plan for their lives. As we read the Gospel of John in a consistent way, seeking God's glory, we begin to see that God wants to be glorified in our lives in spite of the rejection we suffer. If we persevere or "abide" in Jesus's word, our vision becomes clearer, and we may then be able to see that God wants to be glorified *through* the rejection we suffer on his behalf. Let us consider an example from church history that seems to illustrate these points.

Perpetua and Felicity

"My father was so angered by the word 'Christian' that he moved towards me as though he would pluck my eyes out."[1] Around AD 203, a young woman named Vibia Perpetua was sentenced to death for her faith. She had kept a diary of sorts, in which she recorded the trials that led her to the arena of a Roman amphitheatre, where she was torn by wild beasts. On the way to that arena, she suffered much violence, but the first blows she received came from her own father's hand. In her diary, she also describes some of the manipulative techniques her father used as he tried to make her change her mind – that psychological violence hurting almost as much as its physical counterpart.

---

1. The Martyrdom of Saints Perpetua and Felicitas. https://www.ssfp.org/pdf/The_Martyrdom_of_Saints_Perpetua_and_Felicitas.pdf (accessed 18/11/2022).

> This was the way my father spoke out of love for me, kissing my hands and throwing himself down before me. With tears in his eyes he no longer addressed me as his daughter but as a woman. I was sorry for my father's sake, because he alone of all my kin would be unhappy to see me suffer.[2]

At some point, Perpetua, like Jesus, was brought before a Roman governor. And, not unlike Pontius Pilate, this governor noted that the accused person standing before him was a torn individual – rejected by her relatives and separated from her child.

> Hilarianus the governor, who had received his judicial powers as the successor of the late proconsul Minucius Timinianus, said to me: "Have pity on your father's grey head; have pity on your infant son. Offer the sacrifice for the welfare of the emperors."[3]

A Roman judge would not usually have resorted to asking the defendant to do him a favour. But because of Perpetua's noble birth, this governor made an exception – he was nearly begging her to make a pagan sacrifice so that she would be acquitted. But Perpetua refused. Like Jesus before her, she chose to lay down her life (John 10:17–18), not viewing her impending execution as a "tragedy" (see discussion in chapter 3, section titled "Jesus's Death: Not a Tragedy"). She courageously bore testimony to the truth, and she was content to die for that truth. Her father's anger and the adverse circumstances of her life could have been seen as obstacles to healthy Christian discipleship, but she chose to see them as elements of that discipleship. God had given her eyes to see his glory.

As Perpetua followed the one who was rejected by "his own" (John 1:11), she did not complain about being rejected by her "own." Before the wild beasts tore her body, she was already torn from her family and the old ways of life. Before suffering physical death in the arena, she underwent social death. An outcast in her own home, she became a part of the house of God – his glorious temple, destroyed and rebuilt.

That social death involved a radical redrawing of the boundaries marking her social self. Since her father – the most important source of identity in the ancient world – failed to be a spiritual authority figure for her, she lost her status as a privileged Roman and was thrown in prison. But Perpetua, in her diary, also describes the great consolation she received from other Christians

---

2. "Martyrdom."
3. "Martyrdom."

who were sentenced to death like she was. A slave woman named Felicity became her friend – something that would otherwise have been impossible in the strictly differentiated social world of Rome. Separation from one's "own" in the world is usually accompanied by inclusion in a new community of God's "own" – his children born from above. This pattern was present in the life of Jesus and his first disciples, and it is a pattern that is repeated throughout the history of the church.

Perpetua's faith and the encouragement of fellow Christians strengthened her so that she truly overcame the world by her martyrdom. But her account is not triumphalist, and she honestly describes her fear and anxiety:

> A few days later we were lodged in the prison; and I was terrified, as I had never before been in such a dark hole. What a difficult time it was! With the crowd the heat was stifling; then there was the extortion of the soldiers; and to crown all, I was tortured with worry for my baby there.[4]

In her diary, Perpetua freely shares the varied emotions she experienced: fear, anxiety, anger, and sadness. It is normal for a human being to be afraid, angry, or even depressed in the face of adversity. What is missing in her account, however, is surprise. She knew that what was about to befall her would happen according to God's will. Suffering was an indispensable element of her discipleship.

Perpetua is a good example of someone who took seriously Jesus's warning about not being surprised by the world's hatred – one of the main themes of his farewell discourse in the Gospel of John (15:18–20). In this discourse, Jesus also explained that after his departure to the Father, the Holy Spirit would continue his teaching ministry (16:13). Being able to bear adversity for the sake of the word of God is one of the marks of a person whose life has been deeply changed by the Spirit.

One of the things that Jesus, and later the Holy Spirit, wanted to teach his disciples was not to be surprised at the world's hatred. Since false expectations can lead to much confusion and misery in a disciple's life the Spirit, through the word of God, changes, among other things, a person's expectations.

Jesus makes his disciples aware of their own expectations. Not everyone has this kind of awareness. It needs to be cultivated. A disciple's expectations, brought to the light, may have to be corrected, and this correction is likely to

---

4. "Martyrdom."

be a painful process that ultimately results in great liberation. We will look at this idea in the next section.

Expectations

John and another disciple began following Jesus (1:37), literally walking behind him on a path somewhere "across the Jordan" (1:28). Jesus turned and asked them, "What are you seeking?" (1:38) – a question that seems very natural when someone is being followed by two strangers in a deserted place. The two would-be disciples addressed Jesus as "Rabbi" – which means "teacher" – implying that they were willing to learn from him.

In the Gospel of John, the literal and metaphorical meanings of a word are often intertwined, with the metaphorical meaning being deeply rooted in the Hebrew Scriptures. The word "seek" may also mean the general direction of a person's life, and this has to do with what we love and need most, whether or not we are aware of it.

> One thing have I asked of the LORD,
>   that will I seek after:
> that I may dwell in the house of the LORD
>   all the days of my life,
> to gaze upon the beauty of the LORD
>   and to enquire in his temple. (Ps 27:4)

King David, who wrote these words, sought God in a way that still inspires readers today, three thousand years later. Yet, he sought other things in his life, too, and some of those things were very much outside of God's will. When David speaks about himself as having an undivided heart that seeks only to worship the Lord, one could interpret this as poetic exaggeration. Although David often failed to seek God's face, the desire to seek God was certainly present in his heart – even though conflicting with many other desires – and so, God himself called David a man after his own heart (1 Sam 13:14).

The Psalms of David, however, were written not just for David himself but also for the ultimate Son of David – Jesus – whose heart was whole. Unlike fallen human beings, who are disoriented by sin, Jesus sought God's glory with all his heart (John 5:30).

When Jesus asked the two would-be disciples what they were seeking, his question probed deep into their hearts and resonated with desires that they were not even fully aware of. Throughout this gospel, Jesus is portrayed as knowing more about people's hearts than those people themselves (1:47–48;

2:24–25; 6:70–71). The disciples answered with a question that is highly ironic in a Johannine kind of way: "Rabbi . . . where are you staying?" (1:38).

Interpreting this question is similar to peeling an onion – it has layers upon layers of meaning. Perhaps the disciples wanted to know where Jesus was spending the night – maybe whether he was staying somewhere near the camp of John the Baptist. Or perhaps they wanted to know where he lived on a permanent basis. The Greek verb "remain" (μένω, *meno*) that is used here allows for both possibilities. On a deeper level, there is also a hint of another meaning. In a culture where a great deal of information was communicated indirectly, this question indicates the followers' willingness to continue the relationship in a context of hospitality – as either hosts or guests.[5] Jesus accepted this request and invited them to his (temporary) home.

Jesus's answer, however, also has a much deeper meaning, a meaning that would unfold throughout the rest of the Gospel. The disciples would come and see not just his earthly home; eventually, they would see his eternal glory, and it is his will that they stay with him in that glory forever.

The very first words of the Son of God, spoken to his first followers during their first encounter, have to do with their expectations. Throughout the rest of the Gospel, Jesus would do things far exceeding their expectations, yet he will hardly ever fulfil them.

Following Jesus means, among other things, understanding one's expectations, critically analysing them, and being freed from any expectations that are not rooted in God's will. The Gospel of John shows that Jesus taught the disciples to seek God's glory. But sooner or later in this quest, they became aware of the conflict between God's glory and what John calls "the glory that comes from man." This bitter conflict caused and deepened division within Israel (John 7:43; 10:19) and also within the disciples' own hearts. Even believers who have experienced spiritual resurrection – the new birth – still have to struggle with the desire to gain some glory, respect, and recognition from the torn world. That deep-seated desire contributes to false expectations. We see an example of this in the Synoptic Gospels: when Jesus predicted his humiliation, torture, and death (Mark 10:33–34), his disciples were busy competing for prestigious positions in his kingdom as if they had not even heard his predictions (10:35–37). Their expectations were far removed from the reality of his passion.

---

5. Witherington interprets this question as expressing the followers' desire to learn. Witherington, *John's Wisdom*, 70.

In the Gospel of John, this inability to accept Jesus's imminent death and suffering is described in a more nuanced and somewhat ironic way. Shortly before Jesus's last journey to Jerusalem, the disciples expressed concerns over his – and their – safety. According to Carson, "the context makes clear that the disciples did not want to return to Judea. It is not hard to imagine how such fear might well breed a small degree of obtuseness."[6] They had been so traumatized by the attempt of "the Jews" to stone Jesus (John 10:31) that they saw no point in going to Judea: "Rabbi, the Jews were just now seeking to stone you, and are you going there again?" (11:8). The stoning attempt they were referring to had not occurred "just now" but during the feast of Hanukkah – which was celebrated around midwinter – while the conversation reported here took place in spring, not long before Passover. But the disciples' exaggeration is understandable because they were still reeling from shock. They did not expect "the world" to hate Jesus – at least not to that degree.

The modern evangelical movement tends to emphasize "peace with God" – a blessing achieved by faith. While this emphasis has a firm biblical foundation (Rom 5:1), it should not be overemphasized at the expense of other biblical truths. Some evangelicals would be quite uncomfortable speaking about our ongoing conflicts with Christ. The idea of "conflict" does not fit well with their overall approach that is based on contrasting the "before" and the "after" – sinners are in conflict with God before their conversion, but after they come to faith, they have peace with God.

That semantic difficulty disappears, to a large extent, if we maintain the distinction[7] between our union with Christ and our communion with Christ. The former can be understood in terms of "before" and "after"; the latter requires a more nuanced description. In our daily struggles with sin, we are not immune from defeats, which often come when we begin to value something above God's glory. When that happens, we are in conflict with Christ, whether we realize it or not.

In this particular gospel passage, the conflict between Jesus and the disciples is expressed in rather subtle ways, but once these expressions are unpacked, we have a clearer picture. Jesus wanted to go to Judea; the disciples did not. Jesus said, "Let *us* go to Judea" (11:17; emphasis added), and they replied, "Are *you* going there again?" (11:8; emphasis added). Although he referred to Lazarus as "*our* friend," Jesus said, "*I* go to awaken him" (11:11;

---

6. Carson, *Gospel*, 409.

7. This topic was dealt with briefly in chapter 5 (see section titled "Where Does God's Glory Dwell?").

emphasis added). A deeper reason for this conflict has to do with the fact that Jesus acted solely according to the timetable determined by the Father's will (11:6–9), whereas the disciples still lacked the kind of faith that would enable them to understand it; and this faith is referred to as something the disciples still need to grow into (11:15).

Eventually, after Jesus had gently chided them, the disciples gathered the courage to go with him to Judea, but the final resolution of that conflict would have to wait until Jesus was raised from the dead. On that first Easter day, they finally began to understand that the path to glory leads downwards. Watching Jesus arrested and crucified was a terrible experience, but the disciples made it even harder for themselves by holding on to false expectations.

In his last extended conversation with the disciples before his passion, Jesus taught them to have the right expectations about persecution. When he appeared to them after his resurrection, he continued to teach them about persecution and their own expectations. He told Peter to expect a violent death that would, in a paradoxical kind of way, glorify God – not unlike Jesus's own death (21:18–19).

Peter and countless other disciples of Christ died for their faith because they were free from false expectations. In this respect, modern Christians in the Western world often seem to be at a great disadvantage. For us, it is more difficult to accept the idea of our own suffering as a path to glory. The humanistic culture we live in lays great emphasis on improving the world and, thereby, eliminating the need for suffering.

The so-called prosperity gospel – with its extravagant promises of rewards in this life – affects mainstream evangelicalism in more ways than meets the eye. Of course, our leading theologians strongly reject charlatan preachers with their guarantees of a hundredfold income increase to those naïve souls who give them their last savings. Nevertheless, the main premise of the prosperity gospel has its roots in much of modern thinking.

"God wants you to be rich, happy, and successful." This slogan is very attractive because it does contain some truth. In the last chapters of Revelation, we read about the inhabitants of the new Jerusalem as being perfectly healthy and full of joy. The streets of their city are paved with gold, implying that they are rich beyond all measure and all their physical and spiritual needs are taken care of. But that is an image of the future that speaks of the world transformed by the second coming of Christ. The book of Revelation itself makes it clear that the path towards this future glory leads through martyrdom and suffering in this present age.

If we abide in the word of Christ that is recorded in John and other NT texts, we will soon start noticing that there is a conflict in our own hearts. We want to strive for both God's glory and the glory of this age. We want to do God's will, but we want to do so according to our own plans and schedules. We are willing to suffer to some extent for God's kingdom, but we would also like to be able to choose the time and manner of that suffering.

When we begin to follow Christ, we do expect to see God's glory – but we cannot even imagine the greatness of that glory and the unusual, unpredictable ways in which it is manifested. We may also suspect that the path of discipleship will be difficult, but, often, we do not realize how hard it will be. For the disciples in the Gospel of John, God's glory turned out to be infinitely greater than they expected, and the path to that glory turned out to be much more painful than they expected. There is no reason to assume that it should be any different for us.

Sent by the One Sent by the Father

One way to summarize the disciples' expectations and responsibilities is by using the concept of agency. The disciples were freed from many false expectations when they began to see themselves as "sent" into the world (John 20:21).

Jesus sent them into the world because they had already been separated from it; he could not have sent those who still belonged to the world (15:19). The Gospel of Matthew records that Jesus gathered his disciples on a mountaintop – in a liminal space between heaven and earth. But in John, the disciples were given their new identity as witnesses – as "sent ones" – while they were in Jerusalem, hiding in a room with locked doors. There they found themselves in another kind of liminality: "already, but not yet." That liminality was created by Mary Magdalene's testimony, and soon they would go out into the world creating similar liminalities with their testimonies and God's word.

The disciples could now be sent into the world because their new identity had been formed. They understood that they were children of God and brothers of Jesus. They were assured of the forgiveness of their sin and became part of God's renewed temple, and as such were the place where the forgiveness of sins could be communicated to others. They had been given the Holy Spirit, who strengthened them and helped them abide in an ongoing conversation of love with God through Christ. Finally, they had been freed from false expectations and now knew where the path of God's glory might lead them.

The disciples would be physically present in the world, but their spiritual separation from it would not be compromised. Like Jesus, they would be in the world, but not of the world. They would no longer see the world as the source of their origin and identity. From now on, they would see themselves as "sent" into the world. The ability to see oneself in this way is indispensable for a disciple who seeks God's glory.

Torn Mediators for the Torn World

In the history of Christendom, there have been many seekers who tried to separate themselves from the world physically – withdrawing from the world and living in solitude or in closed monastic communities. Such withdrawal, if practised for a limited period, may be a valuable spiritual discipline (Matt 4:1; Mark 6:31), but since followers of Jesus are called to witness in the world, excessive withdrawal may become counterproductive to their mission.

The modern evangelical movement emphasizes the believers' presence in the world, in the public square. But this presence has a redemptive dimension only when there is spiritual otherness and separation from the world. Being actively involved in the affairs of the world goes hand in hand with effective witness to this world only for those Christians who realize their unique identity, which does not originate from the world. When being "in the world" is emphasized at the expense of being "not of the world," the power of Christian testimony may be greatly diminished.

In the Gospel of John, the disciples' identity – in the world but not of the world – can be summed up by the concept of agency – that is, being sent into the world. Let us look at how that concept was understood in ancient Mediterranean cultures. After that, we will see how this concept of agency applies to twenty-first-century situations in which torn disciples of Christ often find themselves.

Before modern means of transportation and communication were invented, distance was perceived in a very different way. Also, the Roman world did not leave much room for social equality. This perception of distance – physical and social – made face-to-face interactions rather rare. Rich and noble Romans did not often communicate directly with their social inferiors – or even with their equals, if these people were far away. Instead, they relied on a network of messengers or agents.

If, for example, the emperor decided to give some land to soldiers who had fought for him, he did not need to meet with them in person. It was enough to send a messenger – a qualified mediator, who would meet with the recipients of the emperor's generosity, discuss their needs and preferences, assess their moral state (whether they would be grateful or discontent upon receiving what was promised), and then return to the palace to report the results of his mission and bring special requests from clients who had asked for favours. It is important to note three features of a successful agent. First, he had to be loyal and trustworthy. He should not seek his own gain. The patron would reward him for his effort, but the agent should not see the clients as a source of material wealth or glory for himself. Second, he had to be competent enough to understand the interests of both the patron and the clients. Third, he should be the kind of person who could move freely between the two social worlds and was able to deal with the distance between these two worlds.[8]

The agent's mission usually began in a high place – for example, the emperor's palace – where he would receive his task. Then he would go down, symbolically, to the world of less noble and privileged clients, and deal with them keeping in mind both their and the patron's interests. The patron was usually interested in gaining greater glory for himself. When that round of interaction with the clients was over, the agent would go back (up) to the palace and report the results. He would share his observations and intercede on behalf of those clients who had special requests. That intercession was usually accompanied by an explanation of how the patron would increase his glory should he choose to honour those requests. The agent's mission was complete only after that report.

These three features of a successful mediator – trustworthiness, competence, and an ability to act in two different social worlds – became even more important in times of conflict. A good example can be found in the autobiography of Josephus. When the Jewish War began, Josephus was appointed commander of one of the rebel groups, but he later surrendered to Vespasian and became his slave. Josephus acted as Vespasian's interpreter and was even entrusted with negotiating with some rebels on behalf of his Roman master.

Josephus described himself as trustworthy, seeking only his master's interest, but also as someone who understood that the peace offer was also good for the rebels. In this way, he sought what was best for both parties. He was competent enough to represent both Rome and the rebels – he spoke their language and understood their mentality since he was one of them not long before. Unfortunately, the rebels failed to see what was best for them. Blinded

---

8. Neyrey, "I am the Door," 276-282.

by unrealistic expectations, they choose to reject Vespasian's offer and thus sealed their fate.

Although a good mediator should be at home in both the social worlds that he deals with, in times of conflict, this is sometimes impossible. Josephus could negotiate with the rebels using his knowledge of their language and culture, but he could never again be one of them – he had burned all his bridges.

This analogy, limited as it is, may help us understand why John, in his gospel, emphasizes Jesus's role as the one sent by God. Jesus is a perfect mediator between God and the torn world. His ministry began at an ontologically high place – he came from the position of God's eternal glory. He descended into the fallen world, bringing the message of God's love for this world. When his ministry was close to completion, he reported to the Father. In his prayer (John 17), he shares the result of his mission – the disciples had come to know the truth, and they would continue to proclaim that truth, eventually attracting new worshippers who will keep glorifying the Father. Jesus interceded for his disciples and for those who would come to faith through their testimony.

In some sense, Jesus's ministry can be deemed complete after that "report." He himself spoke about his victory over the world as of something that had already been accomplished (16:33), even though he still had to go through the agony of the cross. In some other sense, Jesus's earthly ministry was only complete when he ascended to the Father – and there, in that high heavenly place, he continues to intercede for us. Yet, it can also be said that Jesus's ministry is not completed yet and that the disciples, including us, still continue their witness to the world. The "already, but not yet" liminality is also present in heaven.

Every follower of Christ who takes Jesus's words seriously is sent into the world. Not everyone is to be an overseas missionary, literally sent by a church or some sending agency. But the blind man became "sent" when he washed in the "pool of Siloam (which means Sent)" (John 9:7). For John, this play on words is more than just coincidence.

Soon enough, the former blind man discovered this dimension of his new identity – someone who had been "sent." Angry religious fanatics helped him understand this deeper meaning of the name "Siloam." Something similar may happen to us. In times of conflict with "the world," when we are rejected by "our own," we may understand that the roots of that conflict extend all the way to our baptismal pool. As we are baptized in Christ, we begin to share his identity in the world that hated him. We are sent into the world as his messengers, although some of us may need some extra time to come to grips with that reality.

Our task is to be completely loyal to God, seeking to glorify him in his relationship with the torn, rebellious world. We are expected to be competent – to understand both God's word and the world's needs – practising what John Stott called "double listening."[9] Finally, we are to see the rest of our life as a quest for God's glory – a quest that begins with commission, involves going down into the place of the world's misery, and ends with our report and intercessory prayer.

The concept of being "sent" – being in the world but not of the world – shapes our understanding of life as whole, helping us to see our lives not as a tragedy or as the story of a victim. This concept also gives structure to the different segments and periods of our life, and it may help us to establish healthier daily and weekly patterns – beginning with worship in and as God's renewed temple – the community of his children – continuing with witness in the world, and reaching completion with intercessory prayer, in which we can share our observations about what we see in the world.

Thrown or Sent?

I end this chapter with some personal reflections that I hope will be helpful to the readers. As a refugee whose life was torn by war, I try to learn from the experiences of other refugees – in both the first and twenty-first centuries. Dealing with this particular aspect of the brokenness of human life is so challenging that I sometimes feel that no word in my own language can describe it. So I use a German term that has fascinated generations of philosophers and linguists. Perhaps it can be useful for a Bible scholar too.

Like any other language, German has a verb meaning "throw": *werfen*. Like many other languages, German also has a passive form of this verb: *geworfen* – [one that has been] "thrown." The cumbersome genius of this language, however, allows Germans to make nouns out of those passive participle forms: *Geworfenheit* – "the state in which someone realizes that they have been thrown into the world." Some German thinkers – like Heidegger – use this term in a positive sense, to express the sense of wonder – to an inquisitive mind, the world is always full of new and surprising things. But the same word can also be used to describe a situation in which we find ourselves that was not created by our choices or preferences. Thus, the term is applicable to the experience of

---

9. As explained by John Stott in Stott, *The Contemporary Christian: An Urgent Plea for Double Listening*.

people who have been shaken, torn, or forcibly removed from their previous ways of life.

There is no exact equivalent for this word in English – "thrownness" does not quite reflect the depth of meaning of the German term.

As I interact with other refugees in Belgium, I see a lot of this *Geworfenheit* – the feeling of being "thrown" into a world that turns out to be anything but home. I recognize it easily because it has a way of reappearing in my own life too. There is no easy solution to this problem. But the Bible, including the Gospel of John, speaks of people who were thrown into the torn world and then, by God's gracious intervention, restored and sent back into the world. Those who are "thrown" and those who are "sent" experience similar suffering. But those who are "sent" have some hidden resources that help them deal with the suffering.

Can refugees see God's glory in their lives? Some of the characters in the book of Acts would answer, "Yes." When the church in Jerusalem was attacked, this resulted in dispersion, but the dispersion was accompanied by witness (Acts 8:1, 4; 11:19–21). Disciples who had to flee Judea continued to preach the gospel. It was their witness that led to new churches appearing in the lands far from their home. Stephen's death and other acts of violence against the early church resulted in many Christians being "thrown" into a new set of circumstances that were beyond their control. In the book of Acts, the church grows in a paradoxical kind of way: when it is dispersed, it becomes even more fruitful, conquering new lands for God's glory.

This connection between tribulation and growth is also present in the Gospel of John. Jesus came to people who were "thrown" into the world. He set them free and sent them back into the world. In that world, they would suffer greatly, but it is better to suffer as someone "sent" than to suffer as someone "thrown."

If we read the Gospel of John in a consistent kind of way, we can move along the continuum towards becoming more competent readers of that gospel and of the whole Bible. This reading, as it changes our view of Jesus, his death, and the role of Scripture, also corresponds to the shift from being a victim to becoming a conqueror: "For everyone who has been born of God overcomes the world. And this is the victory that has overcome the world – our faith" (1 John 5:4).

Summary

Jesus gives his followers "new eyes" – the ability to interpret reality, including social phenomena. Those disciples who stay faithful to Jesus will realize that their social world is not static but undergoes a radical change as they enter a liminality created by Jesus's words and resurrection. Some – including close relatives – whom they had viewed as authority figures would become outsiders, and some of those who were formerly "out" would now move "in." This principle can be illustrated with the example of Perpetua – a young woman who refused to listen to both her father and the Roman governor when they tried to make her break God's commandment. Those two authority figures became, for her, "outsiders," while a slave woman became her close friend – an "insider." The same pattern can be seen in the life of Jesus: he was rejected by "his own," but God gave him a new community that he called "his own."

God takes care of the faithful disciples of Jesus, and he often does this through other people in their life. The caring, loving community of God's children is part of his response to the challenge of persecution. Within this community, God heals and restores believers who have been traumatized by the world's hatred. When they are restored, he sends them back into the world to witness to his truth.

In order to be God's faithful witnesses in the torn world, disciples of Jesus must analyze their own expectations and reject the so-called prosperity gospel that often comes to them in subtle ways. If they do so, they can act as God's mediators, bringing his message of reconciliation to the world that rebels against him. As mediators, they have to be loyal – not seeking glory for themselves but for God – competent – understanding both God's word and their sociocultural context – and able to transcend boundaries.

Ultimately, being "sent" into the world is more than just a task; it is an important element of our identity. In the Gospel of John, there is a great difference between people who understand that Jesus is sent from God and those who do not. This kind of understanding and confession is the key to grasping the Christological truths revealed in the Gospel of John.

Similarly, understanding one's own identity as someone "sent" into the world makes a great difference in the disciple's life. Being "thrown" out of the synagogue – or some other privileged and protected social or cultural space – is painful. But Jesus transforms "thrown" people into "sent" people. While they still remain torn individuals in a torn world, even in their torn experience they can often see glimpses of future glory. When this happens, they cease to view themselves as victims and begin to think and act as conquerors.

Conclusion

In this book, we have tried to understand John's teaching on suffering and God's glory in our lives. We began with Jesus's puzzling words, spoken shortly before his death: "In the world you will have tribulation. But take heart; I have overcome the world" (John 16:33). We concluded with John's triumphant proclamation: "For everyone who has been born of God overcomes the world. And this is the victory that has overcome the world – our faith" (1 John 5:4). On our way from the first quotation to the second, we dealt with several major themes related to a disciple's identity.

In chapter 1, we looked at John's understanding of "the world." The Fourth Evangelist describes this world as God's creation that rebelled against its Maker. The world is torn between light and darkness, between God's glory and its own desire for independence. God has not given up on this rebellious world but seeks to save it. God's solution to the problem of the world's sin is paradoxical. He chose Israel to be his representative – a torn nation in the torn world.

Israel was also caught in a conflict between its high calling and its failure to live according to that ideal. God renewed Israel in a way that, to outsiders, may seem like destroying it – he allowed the nation to be defeated and taken into captivity. But he also brought Israel back from captivity, and this is how his name was glorified. To communicate this shocking and puzzling truth to his unfaithful people, God raised prophets – torn individuals, who were usually rejected by their fellow citizens, especially the religious leaders. We looked at the example of Isaiah, who preached about God's glory and Israel's renewal through defeat, and noted that the prophet's own life was marked by a somewhat paradoxical attitude to glory and shame.

Similar observation could be made about most other prophets. In the NT, Jesus continued this pattern – he sought God's glory but was rejected by his "own" people. We also noted the importance of studying the historical and literary contexts of the gospels, lest some of their prophetic and polemic features be misunderstood – and sadly, this did happen during some periods in the history of the Western world.

In chapter 2, we sought to answer two foundational worldview questions: "Who are we?" and "Where are we from?" Those questions are important to any thinking person, but for Jewish believers who had been rejected by mainstream Judaism because of their faithfulness to Jesus, these questions became extremely relevant. Russian-speaking Ukrainians whose homes and lives have been wrecked by Russians may also struggle with these questions in a rather intense way. For John the Evangelist, the source of identity of persecuted Christians is God, who had made them his children. The Fourth Gospel has a special emphasis on the theme of adoption and new birth. John explains to his readers who are torn between God's glory and the world's hatred that they are, above all, God's children. They have been born from God's Spirit, and their new birth from the Spirit is connected both to the past – the OT prophecies – and to the future – their hope of the glorious resurrection of the body.

This understanding of new birth results, inevitably, in redrawing the boundaries of the persecuted community. The example of Nicodemus shows that even the leaders of Israel and professional theologians may fail to understand that the OT Scriptures are fulfilled in Jesus and in his followers. The lines between the two communities are drawn, but the outsiders are not without hope. Nicodemus is portrayed as attracted to the light and making remarkable progress. But in order to receive the blessing of salvation, he had to come to Jesus on the terms laid down by God; no one can presume to enjoy God's favour because of any personal achievements or because they belong to some privileged group. An attempt to have a "we-you" relationship with Jesus inevitably fails; but Jesus mercifully invited Nicodemus into an "I-Thou" saving relationship. We also noted that this kind of relationship with Jesus leads to being shamed and rejected by "the world." But this is the only way to escape everlasting shame and destruction in the eschaton.

In chapter 3, we dealt with the third fundamental question of human existence: "Where are we going?" For Jesus and his disciples, their final destiny was God's glory. What is highly unusual, however, is the way that leads to that glory. The story of the blind man (John 9) shows that being rejected by "the world" is not necessarily an obstacle to a healthy spiritual life. Quite the opposite: it is when the former blind man was thrown out of the synagogue that Jesus found him. The whole experience of confrontation with religious leaders, unpleasant as it was, turned out to be a trial that the former blind man successfully endured and overcame by his courageous testimony.

Thereafter, we looked at Jesus's own life and death. His conflict with the religious establishment was much worse – and it led to his crucifixion. But Jesus refused to view his own death as some sort of tragedy, and the Fourth Gospel encourages its readers to interpret Jesus's death as another stage in his quest for God's glory. I tried to show how John's gospel differs from the Synoptics in this respect and how it contributes to a holistic understanding of

Jesus's sacrifice. At the end of chapter 3, we reflected on our ability to see God's glory. The example of Martha shows that much depends on our willingness to focus on God's promises fulfilled in Jesus.

In chapter 4, we considered a situation that seemed to be as far as possible from God's glory – Jesus's crucifixion. For most people living in the Roman Empire, crucifixion was the very opposite of honour. John uses irony to show that what looked like the worst defeat in the eyes of the world is the greatest victory for those who have eyes to see God's glory. The worst kind of shame to which the world could subject Jesus turned out to be the highest expression of God's glory. For Jesus, his resurrection – which, on Good Friday, was still in the future – completely changed the meaning of the cross. In the Gospel of John, the future invades the present; the hope of resurrection shapes our understanding of present trials.

Jesus's resurrection gave his disciples a new perspective, which John shares with his audience. They learned to read the Scriptures in a new, messianic way. The OT became for them not so much a book of rules as a book of promises – promises that had been fulfilled in Jesus. This interpretation of the entire Scripture – as a story of God's faithfulness to his promises – gives meaning to the history of Israel. Difficult as it is, Israel's history is not "tragic"; rather, it is glorious for those who trust the Messiah.

We also discussed some of the difficulties related to reconstructing the initial audience of the Gospel of John. Arguments were offered for a combination of various groups of readers ranging from individuals with only a basic knowledge of Scripture to some very competent interpreters. These groups can be placed along a continuum, and many modern readers would also be able to place themselves on this continuum since the Gospel of John encourages all of us to abide in Jesus's word and to delve deeper and deeper into the Scriptures. In the long run, this kind of reading changes our view of the world and of our own lives. We begin to see ourselves living in a liminality – an "already, but not yet" situation.

The second part of the book (chapter 5 and 6) deals with the disciples' new understanding of the temple, God's glory, and their mission in the torn world. In chapter 5, I described several key features of John's theology of the temple. John sees some continuity between the tabernacle Israel had in the desert, the two temples in Jerusalem (Solomon's and Herod's), Jesus's body, and the community of God's children who are the renewed temple. The presence of God's sanctuary in the midst of sinful people inevitably means a conflict. The Fourth Gospel shows how God provides a solution to this problem.

Every sanctuary Israel ever had was violated in one way or another. The tabernacle was pillaged by the Philistines, and the ark – its most important part – was taken captive. Solomon's Temple was destroyed by the Chaldeans, with God's sacred vessels and his people taken to Babylon. The Second Temple was burned by the Romans. The temple of Jesus's body was crucified. The disciples may expect that the temple formed by their own bodies – and God's Spirit – will also experience violence and rejection. But every instance that God's temple or sanctuary was abused eventually resulted in God's greater glory among the nations.

The disciples are sent into the world to bring glory to God. As the Fourth Gospel shows, one of the chief rivals of this glory is the "glory that comes from man" (John 12:43). John explains, in great detail, that in the torn world, disciples often have to choose between these two kinds of glory.

This choice, to a large extent, shapes the persecuted community that is separated from the world. This separation is not final – the disciples are sent to witness in the world, and their witness creates liminalities – situations where people may still change their allegiance and, instead of glorifying themselves, begin to give glory to God. The last chapter also contained a discussion on the disciples' changed expectations and their role as God's torn messengers in the torn world.

The world's greatest need is to be reconciled to God. Jesus sends his disciples to proclaim this reconciliation. The world will treat them with contempt – just like it treated him with contempt. But it is through suffering, humiliation, and the resurrection of his messengers that God is glorified. This expectation of the glorious future transforms the disciples' present experience so that even when persecuted, they do not have to view themselves as victims. They can think and act as conquerors – here and now.

Selected Bibliography

Beale, G. K. *Handbook on the New Testament Use of the Old Testament*. Grand Rapids: Baker Academic, 2012.
Bonhoeffer, Dietrich. *Life Together*. Reader's Edition. Minneapolis: Fortress, 2015.
Brant, Jo-Ann. *John*. Grand Rapids: Baker Academic, 2011.
Brown, Raymond. *The Community of the Beloved Disciple*. New York: Paulist Press, 1979.
Carson, Donald A. *The Gospel According to John*. Leicester: Inter-Varsity Press; Grand Rapids: Eerdmans, 1991.
Daly-Denton, Margaret. "The Psalms in John's Gospel." In *The Psalms in the New Testament*, edited by Steve Moyise and Maarten J. J. Menken, 119–36. London; New York: T&T Clark, 2004.
Frankl, Viktor E. *Man's Search for Meaning*. New York: Washington Square, 1959.
Hanson, Anthony Tyrell. *The Prophetic Gospel: A Study of John and the Old Testament*. Edinburgh: T&T Clark, 1991.
Huntington, Samuel P. *The Clash of Civilizations and the Remaking of World Order*. New York: Simon & Schuster, 1996.
Ignatius of Loyola. *The Spiritual Exercises of St. Ignatius*. Translated by Anthony Mottola. Garden City: Image Books, 1964.
Jenkins, Philip. *The New Faces of Christianity: Believing the Bible in the Global South*. Oxford: Oxford University Press, 2008.
Josephus, Flavius. *The Works of Flavius Josephus*. 4 vols. Translated by William Whiston. Grand Rapids: Baker Book House, 1974.
Keener, Craig S. *The Gospel of John: A Commentary*. 2 vols. Peabody: Hendrickson, 2003.
Koester, Craig R. "The Spectrum of Johannine Readers." In vol. 1 of *What Is John? Readers and Reading of the Fourth Gospel*, edited by Fernando F. Segovia, 5–19. SBL Symposium Series 3. Atlanta: Scholars Press, 1996.
———. *The Word of Life: A Theology of John's Gospel*. Grand Rapids: Eerdmans, 2008.
Kok, Jacobus (Kobus). *New Perspectives on Healing, Restoration and Reconciliation in John's Gospel*. Biblical Interpretation Series 149. Leiden; Boston: Brill, 2017.
Köstenberger, Andreas J. "The Destruction of the Second Temple and the Composition of the Fourth Gospel." *TJ* 26 (2005): 205–42.
———. "Jesus as Rabbi in the Fourth Gospel." *BBR* 8 (1998): 97–128.
———. *John*. Baker Exegetical Commentary on the New Testament. Grand Rapids: Baker Academic, 2004.
Leithart, Peter J. *Revelation 12–22*. New York: Bloomsbury T&T Clark, 2018.
Lewis, C. S. *Mere Christianity*. San Francisco: Harper, 2001.
Martyn, James Louis. *History and Theology in the Fourth Gospel: A New Testament Literary Classic*. 3rd ed. Louisville: Westminster John Knox, 2003.

Menken, Maarten J. J. "The Significance of the OT in John." In *Theology and Christology in the Fourth Gospel: Essays by the Members of the SNTS Johannine Writings Seminar*, edited by G. Van Belle, J. G. Van der Watt, and P. J. Maritz. 155–75. Leuven: Leuven University Press, 2005.

Motyer, Stephen. *Your Father the Devil?: A New Approach to John and 'the Jews.'* Carlisle: Paternoster, 1997.

Moyise, Steve. *The Old Testament in the New: An Introduction*. 2nd ed. London: Bloomsbury T&T Clark, 2015.

Musurillo, Herbert, trans. *The Acts of the Christian Martyrs*. Edited by Henry Chadwick. London: Oxford University Press, 1972. https://www.ssfp.org/pdf/The_Martyrdom_of_Saints_Perpetua_and_Felicitas.pdf (accessed 18/11/2022).

Neyrey, Jerome H. *The Gospel of John in Cultural and Rhetorical Perspective*. Grand Rapids; Cambridge, UK: Eerdmans, 2009.

———. "'I Am the Door' (John 10:7, 9): Jesus the Broker in the Fourth Gospel." CBQ 69 (2007): 270–291.

Schuchard, Bruce G. *Scripture within Scripture: The Interrelationship of Form and Function in the Explicit Old Testament Citations in the Gospel of John*. SBLDS 133. Atlanta: Scholars Press, 1992.

Stott, John. *The Contemporary Christian: An Urgent Plea for Double Listening*. Leicester: Inter-Varsity Press, 2002.

Witherington, Ben, III. *John's Wisdom: A Commentary on the Fourth Gospel*. Louisville: Westminster John Knox, 1995.

Wright, N. T. *The Resurrection of the Son of God*. Minneapolis: Fortress, 2003.

Langham

Langham Literature and its imprints are a ministry of Langham Partnership.

Langham Partnership is a global fellowship working in pursuit of the vision God entrusted to its founder John Stott –

> *to facilitate the growth of the church in maturity and Christ-likeness through raising the standards of biblical preaching and teaching.*

Our vision is to see churches in the Majority World equipped for mission and growing to maturity in Christ through the ministry of pastors and leaders who believe, teach and live by the word of God.

Our mission is to strengthen the ministry of the word of God through:
- nurturing national movements for biblical preaching
- fostering the creation and distribution of evangelical literature
- enhancing evangelical theological education

especially in countries where churches are under-resourced.

Our ministry

Langham Preaching partners with national leaders to nurture indigenous biblical preaching movements for pastors and lay preachers all around the world. With the support of a team of trainers from many countries, a multi-level programme of seminars provides practical training, and is followed by a programme for training local facilitators. Local preachers' groups and national and regional networks ensure continuity and ongoing development, seeking to build vigorous movements committed to Bible exposition.

Langham Literature provides Majority World preachers, scholars and seminary libraries with evangelical books and electronic resources through publishing and distribution, grants and discounts. The programme also fosters the creation of indigenous evangelical books in many languages, through writer's grants, strengthening local evangelical publishing houses, and investment in major regional literature projects, such as one volume Bible commentaries like *The Africa Bible Commentary* and *The South Asia Bible Commentary*.

Langham Scholars provides financial support for evangelical doctoral students from the Majority World so that, when they return home, they may train pastors and other Christian leaders with sound, biblical and theological teaching. This programme equips those who equip others. Langham Scholars also works in partnership with Majority World seminaries in strengthening evangelical theological education. A growing number of Langham Scholars study in high quality doctoral programmes in the Majority World itself. As well as teaching the next generation of pastors, graduated Langham Scholars exercise significant influence through their writing and leadership.

To learn more about Langham Partnership and the work we do visit **langham.org**

Milton Keynes UK
Ingram Content Group UK Ltd.
UKHW022123040424
440549UK00015B/656

9 781839 739279